Increase Your Mobile DJ Business by 30%
... Starting Next Month!

by Bob Popyk

Increase Your Mobile DJ Business by 30% ... *Starting Next Month!*

Copyright ©1998 by Bentley-Hall, Inc.

All rights reserved.

Printed in the United States of America.

ISBN 1-890614-01-7

No part of this publication may be reproduced, stored in a retrieval system or transmitted in any form or by any means (electronic, mechanical, photocopy, recording or otherwise) without the express prior written permission of the copyright owner.

Edited by Kristen Simpson
Designed by Antoinette Follett
Illustrations by Gerry Stockley

For information on ordering more copies of this book, or to receive a free sample issue of the *Creative Selling*® newsletter, contact Bentley-Hall, Inc., 120 Walton Street, Suite 201, Syracuse, New York 13202-1211, phone (800) 724-9700, fax (800) 724-3881.

This book is intended for use by professional mobile DJs. The procedures and advice herein have been shown to be appropriate for applications described; however, no warranty (expressed or implied) is intended or given. Moreover, the user of this book is cautioned to be familiar with sales and customer service practices and procedures.

First Edition

Printing number

10 9 8 7 6 5 4 3 2 1

Contents

Chapter 1
Getting Started 1

Chapter 2
Where Is Your Next Gig Coming From? 4
    Who's in the News?
    Personal Promotion from Your Pocket or Purse
    A Personal Approach to Direct Mail
    Tips For Producing a Direct Mail Promotion
    When You Do Advertise

Chapter 3
There's a Customer on Line Two 26
    First You Need to Find Out Who's Calling
    When the Customer Asks the Price Over the Phone

Chapter 4
A Different Look at Shows 40
    Attracting Buyers to Your Display
    What Happens When People Do Stop?
    Using Freebies

Chapter 5
What Ever Happened to ... ? 50

Chapter 6
Turning Leads into Sales 56
    Have a Plan and a Goal
    Follow Up Regularly
    Using the Phone
    Every Prospect Is Different
    Following Up Leads with Direct Mail
    Mailing Lists
    Other Ideas
    People Who Book the Competition
    Follow-Up Does Work

Chapter 7
Bringing Them Back Alive 68
    Don't Forget to Say "Thank You"

Chapter 8
Basic Creative Sales Skills Are a Necessity 75
    Recognizing That If You Can't Close, Nothing Else You
        Do Right Matters
    Qualifying Tie-Downs
    The Art of Conversation
    Compliment Your Way to a Sale
    You Need Better-Than-Basic Sales Skills
    Cleaning Up the Sale
    Rejection

Chapter 9
Overcoming Objections 88
Objections You'll Probably Hear
Objection Categories
Confronting Price-Value Objections
20 Things to Do Before Cutting the Price
Legitimate Objections
Handling Indecision

Chapter 10
Referral Selling and "Who Do You Know?" 106
Turning Clients into Torchbearers
Networking: The Power of Personal Contact

Chapter 11
Customer Service as a Sales Tool 119
Attitude Really Makes the Difference
Customer Service Builds Loyalty
Self-Analysis
Customer Service as Insurance

Chapter 12
Putting Your Plan into Action 141

Introduction

I am not a DJ. I don't pretend to be one. What I am, though, is your customer. I've booked a lot of DJs over the years. A while back, I was made the entertainment chairman of the country club I've belonged to for more than 20 years. The reason for the appointment was obvious. Nobody else wanted the job.

Although I resisted hiring DJs at first, I eventually came to see how many times they would bring more than a band could: light shows, fog machines, comedy, audience involvement, and so on. Initially we never booked a DJ. Now we hire a DJ for 65 percent of our parties. And if you're good, we have you back.

Increasing your mobile DJ business by 30 percent next month may sound like an impossible goal to many DJs. But it's very possible ... if you have the initiative, some assertiveness, a little creativity, and a plan.

How long have you been in business? One year, two years, five years? Have you been in business 10 years or more? If you've been around for awhile, you've probably seen good years and bad years, economy fluctuations and changes in customer demands. If you're new in the DJ business, you're going to find that nothing will be the same year after year. As things change, you have to change with them. You can't do the same thing day after day, month after month, year after year and expect to increase your business as a result.

If you want to increase your DJ business by 30 percent next month, you have to do something *this* month. That's the catch. It won't happen by itself. You have to make it happen. And you have to *want* to do it. How badly do you want to increase your business? How hard are you willing to work? What sacrifices will you make? Remember the old adage: The harder you work, the luckier you get.

This book contains many suggestions and ideas for increasing your mobile DJ business right away. Take the ones you like the best and give them a try. Will they work? You won't know until you give it a shot and find out for yourself. It's all up to you. Just a few ideas put to use could have some dramatic results. You might find that your business will increase substantially sooner than next month!

—Bob Popyk

1

In the middle of every difficulty lies opportunity.

—Albert Einstein

Getting Started

There are a lot of ways to increase your mobile DJ business. For example, you could:

- Double your advertising budget.
- Reduce your prices drastically.
- Open a location in another city.

But that's *not* what this book is about. It's about making more money, not spending it. It's about taking the resources you already have and putting them to better use. In fact, you may find that you can increase your mobile DJ business while spending *less* than you're accustomed to.

Where do you start? Go get a legal pad and a pencil. This will be easier than you think. Draw a line down the middle of a page. On one side write: "things to do," and on the other side write: "people to call." Now, as you read this book, make some notes. You'll find that after just a few chapters, you'll start to develop a game plan that you can put to use *this* month to increase your business *next* month. And while you're doing it, you'll have a

You Can't Do It Alone

One of the easiest steps you can take toward increasing your business is hiring more DJs. After all, you can only be in one place at a time. But if you add one other DJ, you just doubled the number of gigs your company can handle. Pay the DJs a set rate per gig, keeping a cut of the revenue for yourself.

Where to find DJs? Networking is the key. Try radio stations, musicians, college students, clubs, friends, and acquaintances. It's very important that you have a good understanding of your DJs' personalities, so you'll be able to assign them to jobs where they'll have the best fit. You probably won't want to send the 60-year-old guy who does well spinning oldies at 50th anniversary parties to a high school dance. A young DJ more in touch with current music would be a better fit.

Just as you don't have to handle all of the gigs you get yourself, you also don't have to own every piece of equipment you may need. Some of your customers may ask for special effects like fog, confetti guns, and so forth. Save yourself some money by renting, leasing, or borrowing the equipment you need, until you get enough requests for it that it will pay for itself. Factor your rental costs into the price you quote.

chance to put down the names of some customers and prospects to call, too.

Getting started with a plan to increase your mobile DJ business means making the most out of every single incoming call, looking for referrals, creating new prospects, staying in touch with previous customers, following up leads and possibly bringing your sales skills up a notch. Don't forget about customer service. That's really a great sales tool if you know how to implement it and use it. After that, it's just a matter of putting your plan into action.

Everybody has their own routine for finding more gigs. What do you do? Think about it over coffee in the morning? Wait for customers to call? Think about it while you're at lunch? I bet that if you changed your routine just a little bit to focus on finding more customers to talk to, your bookings would change for the better as well.

It's a simple formula:

More Prospects/Customers = More Bookings

Too basic? Well, the more people you talk to about your DJ services, the more bookings you'll get. Each day, you want to concentrate just a few minutes on where your next customer is coming from. Take a look at your legal pad. Who do you write to? Who do you call? Let's get started by thinking about where your next gig might be coming from ...

2

Determine that the thing can and shall be done, then we shall find the way.

—Abraham Lincoln

Where Is Your Next Gig Coming From?

To increase your business by 30 percent, you have to have a plan. You can't just sit back and wait for customers to come flocking to you or to start ringing your phone off the hook: you need to have a strategy for attracting them. This is the key to your entire effort. Spend some time developing a game plan of how you're going to attract those new customers. Where are they going to come from? How are they going to hear about you? How are you going to get them to call you?

Most mobile DJs answer these questions with one word: advertising. Need more bookings? Advertise. Want people to know about your DJ service? Advertise. Unfortunately, most of the ads they come up with don't stand out. Think about it. A service, a price, a business name. Those are the ads in any business, whether you're advertising DJ services or carpet cleaning. But, advertising isn't the only answer for finding more customers.

Maybe a little more creative marketing could bring in a few more bookings. Maybe you need more than a service, a price, and a business name.

Let me tell you a little story. My parents grew up during the Depression. Neither one of them had much of an education. Both of them were factory workers, and they came from a strong ethnic background. They also had some common sense for survival.

Money was tight after World War II, and in the late '40s, every once in a while my parents would sell something using the classified ads in the daily paper. It didn't matter if they were selling a car or an appliance; my parents had a marketing strategy.

They would make the item they were selling sound as interesting as possible, then list our address. Never a phone number, just an address. I asked my father once why he didn't list our phone number, and he said, "If you want to sell something, you've got to meet the people first. If they call, they'll find a reason not to come. Once they're here, I've got a better chance that they'll buy."

That's the first rule of selling: *You have to meet people face-to-face.*

My parents had an acre of land, and they grew their own vegetables, grapes, and strawberries. We always had a lot of strawberries, so we sold the extras by the side of the road. We lived on the main road coming into town, and there was always a lot of traffic.

I had the job of manning the card table by the road to sell the strawberries. I kind of liked doing that because it sure beat having to pick them all day. I hated picking. So I would sit on my stool in back of the card table that was loaded with strawberries. The only advertising I had was a piece of cardboard that read: "Strawberries 4 Sale."

People would drive up and ask, "How much?" I'd say, "50 cents a quart," and they'd drive off. So I asked my mom: "Why can't I put the price on the sign so they'd know how much the strawberries are before they pull over?"

She said: "Then fewer people would pull over. It's up to you to get them to buy after they stop."

I thought about this for a while, and then when somebody stopped and asked "How much?" I'd say "Two quarts for a dollar," and let them talk me into selling them just one quart. I'd always sell the whole table in time to watch Captain Video on our brand-new TV set.

So that's the second rule of selling: *You have to establish an interest and a need; and the value has to exceed the price.*

But sometimes I'd give a pitch and give a price, and the people would drive off. Then I found that if they asked how much, and I gave my little spiel, hit them with a price and then said, "How many would you like?" I would sell twice as many twice as fast, just because I asked them to buy.

The third rule of selling: *If you don't ask, you don't get.*

Now, all of this may sound pretty basic to you. But my parents could sell a car with a $1 classified ad. They could sell a lot of quarts of strawberries without cutting their prices. They knew how to find customers and get them to buy—without a marketing degree. It just took some common sense.

There are things you can do to find more customers, without increasing your overhead or doubling your advertising budget.

How about this: let's pull together the names of:

- Three previous customers you haven't seen for a while.
- Three prospects who called but didn't book you.

That's six people total, and each of your employees can make one of these lists.

Now, first you call the three people you haven't seen for a while and ask how they're doing. Tell them that you have some new music or equipment that just arrived, and you'd like to invite them over to see or hear whatever it is just to get their opinion on it. (People love to give opinions, and it's easier than asking them to spend money.)

Then call the three people who didn't book you when they called and try to get them to meet with you one more time. Offer them a special gift or freebie. Tell them about something they may have missed. Figure out what it will take for a face-to-face meeting once more this week.

That's six calls—six contacts that won't take very long. Multiply that by five days a week, and that's 30 customer contacts per week. If you did that on a regular basis, you'd have more than 120 new customer contacts EACH MONTH! If just a small percentage of those people called or came to your office, you'd never be lacking for people to talk to about bookings.

Who's in the News?

Newspapers can provide invaluable information to mobile DJs. Make it a practice for you or someone on your staff to check the area newspapers every day for listings of engagements. Come up with a simple "Congratulations on your engagement" letter you can mail to everyone on these lists inviting them to stop into your office or give you a call. Offer them a small gift as an added incentive for coming by or calling. Your reader should also watch for stories on upcoming reunions, dances, and other events that will require or could benefit from the services of a mobile DJ.

Personal Promotion from Your Pocket or Purse

Finding more business takes a certain amount of personal advertising. This starts with those little billboards you carry around in your pocket. You read stories about salespeople who carry around thousands of business cards, take them to football games, and throw them up in the air when a team scores a touchdown. Or they plaster them in restaurants and car washes, or give them out 12 at a time. These make great stories, but the effectiveness of these techniques is questionable at best.

How do you use your business cards? Do they sit idly in your desk drawer, only to be tossed out when your phone number changes? Or do they come out of your pocket as soon as your client says, "I'm going to think about it?" Are they great for picking your teeth or writing notes to yourself on the back? Or do they help you create more business or bring customers back one more time?

Check your business cards. Are they current? Do they have all the up-to-date information on how to reach you? Do your cards have your fax number, your cell phone number, your e-mail address? Do they have information about your Web site? Are they a good representation of your services and yourself? When you give out a card, does it look brand new, or does it look like it's been used once or twice before?

An e-mail address on a business card shows that you're keeping up with the times. Listing fax and cell phone (or pager) numbers shows that you're very accessible. And a card that isn't stained or dog-eared shows that you are concerned with quality and appearance. But that's just the beginning. How you put them to use is just as important as the look of the cards themselves. Some mobile DJs take their cards to another level. There's a DJ in Idaho whose business card has a fold-over with a perforated edge that becomes a discount coupon. A DJ in Mexico has a business card that is folded in a unique way to make it stand up when it's set on something. He puts them on all the tables at events he works.

How about the back of your business cards? Is this space used at all? Several DJs use the reverse side of their cards to print some of the special equipment and services they offer. Another DJ uses the back of his card to list his Web page URL and e-mail address, plus a small version of his home page.

With the amount of phone numbers and other information you might want to list on your business card, don't make the mistake of trying to cram it all onto one side. That's why the fold-over card with three to four sides of usable space is an option.

One rule of thumb is to make sure that you can put a quarter somewhere on your business card without covering any type. If there isn't enough blank space to set a quarter on it somewhere, you may be overdoing it. So before you put your company slogan, the number of years you've been in business, five phone, fax, and cellular numbers, and a list of all the different kinds of events you handle on one side of your business card, think about your company image, the possibility of confusing the customer, and whether your business card will stand out from your competition's.

Something else. You can have different cards for different uses. Maybe you want a card with a coupon for bridal shows and other outside events. You may have another card to give to interested prospects you meet while on a gig.

This does not mean that you have to spend thousands of dollars on business cards. Some of the most creative forms require little or no money. In fact, one DJ in New Jersey seldom gives out his regular card. When a prospect tells him she's "going to think about it" and asks for his card, he says he doesn't "have one at his fingertips." Then he pulls out his checkbook and rips a check in half so just the business name, address and phone number are on it. He writes his name on the bottom and says, "use this." It really gets customers' attention.

A DJ in Wisconsin says that he doesn't like to have business cards that are the same shape and size as all of his competitors', so when a customer asks for his card, he takes out a 3" x 5" index card and writes his name, address, and phone number on it. He says that it really stands out from the little stack of regular business cards the customer has been accumulating from other DJs. It's certainly a lot bigger, doesn't get lost, and has a personal touch. And when he writes, "I want to earn your business!" in longhand, it really means something.

Here are some creative uses of business cards that really work:

- Have a rubber stamp made that says, "This card is good for one free..." (It could be an extra half hour on a four-hour gig.) Stamp the back of your card and send it to a prospect when you need to get him or her to call back one more time.
- Leave a business card with a tip in a restaurant. Maybe the waiter or waitress, or someone he or she knows, needs the services of a mobile DJ.
- Staple a business card to every check that you mail with a bill. You're paying for postage anyway, so you might as well get some exposure. Somebody on the other end has to handle that card, even if only to throw it away. They'll probably take a minute to look at it. This is free exposure that just might pan out.

Where Is Your Next Gig Coming From?

After I wrote a column in *Mobile Beat* about business cards, we received a ton of letters and phone calls from people who had interesting and clever business cards and from a number of people who had ways to use them creatively to find new customers, bring in a lead, or turn a sale around. One DJ's business card looked like a baseball trading card. Another sent me a card that looks like a small book. Another had a business card with a map to her office on the back.

I had a number of calls from people who always give out two cards when someone asks for one. They simply ask the person to give the extra one to a friend. There also was a long list of people who made sure the reverse side of the business card was left blank, in spite of filling up the front with phone, fax, and cellular numbers and e-mail addresses. Several salespeople said they always wrote, "I want to earn your business" on the back of the card when giving it out. Nice touch. The person who sent me the business card with the words "Rent this space" on the back might not grab a lot of business from his customers, but he did get a chuckle from me.

More and more people seem to be putting their pictures on their business cards. If you're photogenic, it might be the way to go. If you're not, it's still something to consider. Beauty is in the mind of the beholder.

Color stands out on business cards. Gold leaf does, too. Five-color is better than four-color, and two or three color stands out better than just plain black and white. Raised letters don't seem to make the impression they may have years ago, and parchment or unusual card stock may take the risk of bending or soiling easily.

One of the things should never do if you want to make a good impression is take somebody else's business card, cross off his name, and write yours over it. If someone is thinking about spending a lot of money with you for a wedding gig, writing your name in on a business card with a stubby pencil before you give your prospect a card does not present the image of a solid, experienced, in-it-for-the-long-haul DJ.

If you're using your business cards in a way that makes it easy for customers to get away from you, you might want to rethink the whole process. And if your business card is out-of-date or very ordinary, you might want to take a long look at what it would take to make it a good reflection of your business.

There's one other important thing to remember about business cards—always have some with you. Remember, you never know when you might run into someone looking for a DJ. Be sure to have plenty with you at every gig. Just keep them behind your board, where you can easily reach them when someone asks for one.

Business cards can bring business in, they can bring customers back, and they can be one of the best methods of personal advertising you have. Take a look at some of the business cards you have collected yourself. If your business card doesn't match their uniqueness and go beyond their creativity, now's the time to do something about it.

A Personal Approach to Direct Mail

How did your last direct mail piece do? When you sent out your last mailer or flier, how much response did you get? Did your customer, prospect or addressee actually open your envelope to read your print piece? Think about this for a minute. What do you do with the mail that comes to you each morning? Do you sort it standing over a wastebasket? Do you think to yourself: "Junk mail (trash), another letter from Publisher's Clearing House (trash), AOL solicitation (trash), American Express bill (keep), bulk-mail ad piece (trash), personal letter with 32-cent stamp (keep)," and so on? You're not alone. So how do you know those next 100, 500, or 5,000 envelopes you send out promoting your mobile DJ business are even going to get opened? First you have to get your prospects' attention.

I received a direct-mail piece the other day that had on the outside of the envelope the words: "This is not another letter from Ed McMahon." Clever idea. I opened the envelope, read it, then threw it away. But at least I read it first. They had their shot at me. And that's what direct mail is all about. If your prospects or customers don't open the envelope, if they don't read what's inside, you're spinning your wheels. So, how do you get people to give you their attention, even if it's just for a few seconds?

The easiest way to see what works is to go through your mail in the morning and see what gets your attention. What makes you want to open an envelope and read something? First of all, you may notice that any personal-size envelope, with an address written in longhand and a 32-cent stamp attached, gets opened right away. Bulk mail doesn't. Any letter that looks like it might be from one of your friends and not a bill or solicitation, gets opened right away. Postcards get looked at right away, because you don't have to open an envelope. Start to see any similarity? If it looks like junk mail, it probably is junk mail. If it looks important, it probably is. So the idea, I guess, is to make your piece not look like junk mail. Make it look important. Get their attention.

It also depends on how many people you're sending your direct-mail piece to. If you are targeting a smaller audience, you probably can spend more and be more creative. I'm amazed at the way some companies and individuals are getting people's attention.

Roland Musical Instruments sent a direct-mail piece out to their dealers informing them of an upcoming dealer meeting. They wanted to make sure it didn't get lost in the midst of their dealers' other mail that day, so they sent it in the form of a space gun. They actually bought the guns retail and had them customized, printed and reboxed. They were in the shape of a spaceship that shot out little foam disks when you pulled the trigger. They made a great sound, and the disks flew about 30 feet. When you picked the disks up, the names of the Roland products and other information were on them. The theme was "new product launch." No one threw the toys away. Everybody played with them. They caught everybody's attention.

There's a sales consultant who sends a baseball bat with his name engraved on it to people considering using his services. It's a real Louisville Slugger, and the card with the bat suggests using the consultant as a "heavy hitter" to help close more sales. He certainly gets your attention with that bat. After you take it out of the box, you've got to put it somewhere. You certainly can't toss the bat in the wastebasket—the basket would tip over. The consultant even puts his phone number on the bat so you'll know where to call.

One advertising agency sends a birdhouse to prospective clients. The note reads: "From our house to your house ... we do it all in-house." Neat idea.

Get this one. If the city of Rochester, New York, thinks you might like to hold a meeting or convention there, they'll mail you one of those Kodak single-use cameras (made in Rochester) just to make sure you read through their letter.

To get a prospect's attention, sometimes you hardly have to spend anything. What you really want to do is get some kind of response without spending a whole lot of money.

I know of a music dealer who sent out hundreds of letters announcing an upcoming concert and clinic. In his rush to get the 2,000-piece mailing out, 100 envelopes were accidentally sent out empty. Sixty of the 100 people who got empty envelopes called the store to find out what was in them. Each person was told of the haste in sending out the letters, and were asked to come and to bring a friend with them. The place was packed.

Wood Mode Kitchens sent all their distributors a cassette tape in an envelope informing them of a new sales campaign. On the outside of the envelope were the words: "This tape will self-destruct in five minutes." Everybody played the tape. It got their attention.

One of the more successful car salespeople in the country sends out 10 postcards a day to his past prospects and customers with the words: "Trying to reach you, please give me a call." That simple. Nothing more. It averages an 80 percent response rate because of people's curiosity as to why they should call. It gets their attention.

A salesperson in a Sea Ray boat dealership tries to get a prospect back in one more time by sending a letter with 16 stamps on it. They are all two-cent stamps. Everyone else sticks 32-cent stamps on their envelopes or runs them through a meter. His letter stands out. It always gets opened.

A well-known copywriter got his newsletter off the ground by sending a letter with a dollar bill taped inside. The next words were, "I want to get you used to receiving money in the mail." It got my attention. I kept the dollar bill and spent $179 to subscribe.

Everyone has received a letter that states, "You may have already won ... " but nothing beats, "You have already won!" How badly do you want more customers? Can you afford to give away something small to do it? Is it worth a few dollars to talk to a potential customer?

It takes more to get a customer's attention today than ever before. If you're going to rely on mundane, run-of-the-mill advertising, you'd better be ready to compete with every local small business owner, from your neighborhood Amway distributor to the Ziebart dealer, to get customers' attention.

Drive down the street, and the billboards scream: "Buy! Buy! Buy!" Open the daily paper, and the ads scream: "Buy from ME! Buy from ME!" Look through your mail, and Dick Clark asks you to buy magazines, direct-mail catalogs try to sell like there's no tomorrow, and in the middle of all of this, you're out there vying for the American dollar. And you're not going anywhere until you get noticed. You've got to get your customers' attention. Sometimes it's just a matter of being a little more clever.

There's no magic formula for getting a prospect's or customer's attention in an advertising or promotional campaign. Take a look at what other industries are doing, and capitalize on the things you like the best. From now on, don't throw away your junk mail; save it, read it, and see what techniques you could apply to your own mailings. Getting your customer's attention first will make sure your message has a chance. A little creativity goes a long way.

Tips For Producing a Direct Mail Promotion

First, you have to decide what kind of format you're going to use. Direct-mail advertising offers you a virtually unlimited choice of formats.

- **The classic format** uses an outer envelope enclosing a promotional brochure. It is generally accompanied by a separate letter as well.

- **The self-mailer** does not have an outer envelope. It is generally less expensive than the "classic format."
- **The catalog** is a great direct mail piece.
- **Special devices** can be included in a direct mail package. Examples are rub-offs, stamps, pop-ups, and tokens.
- **The invitation** is a very effective method of getting the attention of prospects. It prompts the reader to take action.

When sending any direct-mail piece, always provide a way for people to respond—a card, a telephone number, or both.

Write a "grabber" letter. What you say and how you say it is everything in direct-mail advertising. Make sure to promise a benefit in your headline or first sentence. Then go on to give more information about that benefit. Tell the reader exactly what you are offering. Be sure to repeat your most important points in the closing paragraph and then prompt the reader to take some sort of immediate action. A clever P.S. can help as well. (A handwritten P.S. is the most-read portion of many direct-mail pieces.)

Make your letter look appealing and professional. Do this by keeping your paragraphs short, using subheads, and emphasizing important points by using bold or italic type, capital letters, or color.

Sometimes it's tough to come up with a good reason for sending direct mail. You want to keep in contact with customers and prospects, but it can be hard to find the right pull. Here are a couple of ideas for getting prospects to contact you.

- **Invite them to a party.** Offer free refreshments, activities, and door prizes. Be sure to mention the refreshments. Have your MCs, DJs, dancers and any other performers you use perform. Display your lighting equipment, props, etc. You may want to offer special buying incentives.

- **Write a newsletter.** Many DJs have found that newsletters are a great way to keep in contact with prospects and customers. Most people honestly enjoy getting newsletters from businesses if they include information about certain events, new developments, party-planning tips, and so forth. By keeping abreast of local news and putting together a few simple articles, you can provide a service for your customers and keep your name in front of them.

- **Send them postcards.** The next time you're on vacation or out of town for business, get a stack of postcards at the hotel's front desk. Send them to your hottest prospects and best customers with a note saying something like, "I'm here in Las Vegas at a DJ convention (or whatever) and I just got an idea that I think would be great for your next corporate party! I can't wait to talk to you as soon as I get back." When you call them when you get back from your trip, they'll be happy to hear from you, because you thought of them while you were away. Not bad for a 20-cent or 32-cent postage investment.

Here's a simple tip that can sometimes make a difference without any additional cost at all. Third-class stamps can make your bulk mail look more like it's first class. Bulk rate stamps are used just like first-class stamps, but the letters or flats must be presorted according to postal regulations. If you currently use a bulk rate permit, you can continue to sort your mailings as you have in the past.

Bulk rate stamps can be ordered and purchased from your post office. If you don't currently use bulk rate services, your local post office can help you analyze the benefits. Bulk rate stamps can help you keep costs down while improving mailing response rates with a first-class look.

When You Do Advertise

This book is about increasing your business without increasing your expenses, so I won't go into a lot of detail about traditional advertising. However, there are some things you can do to advertise your mobile DJ services in traditional media without spending the traditional large amounts of money.

The least expensive time to advertise, especially on the radio, is during the months of January, February, and March. The holidays are over and retailers are cutting back on their advertising. That means radio stations are hurting for advertisers. It just happens that this is also one of the best times for DJs to advertise to the wedding market. So plan a radio advertising campaign for this time of year, then negotiate with your local stations for the best rates.

You may even be able to barter for advertising space instead of paying cash. Offer to trade a DJ and sound system for a radio station's special event, or a DJ for a newspaper Christmas party in exchange for advertising space. If you go this route, you'll probably want to concentrate on one radio station or newspaper, so you can build up enough barter credit to make your campaign worthwhile. Remember, one ad makes much less of an impact than a series of ads. Most people don't remember an advertising message until they've been exposed to it many times.

Coupons are always popular. Consider placing an offer in the coupon section of your city's Yellow Pages. Most people looking for a DJ turn first to the phone book—your coupon could be the touch that makes them call you instead of a competitor.

Another new place for coupons is the Internet. If you have a Web site, place a coupon on a page instructing prospects to print it out and bring it to their meeting with you. The World Wide Web is attracting more and more users every day. Many people plan entire vacations on the Web, buy a car through the Internet, and some even meet their future spouses this way. Why not find a DJ online? The Internet represents a whole new market for you.

Questions & Thought-Starters

Think about the following, and jot down some answers on your legal pad.

1) Outline your plan for attracting new customers as it stands right now. What are you going to do to get your name out there? How are more people going to hear about you and your DJ service?

2) What are the three basic rules for getting more bookings?

3) How can you use your local newspaper to increase business (other than running another ad)?

4) List three things you can do to get more use out of your business cards.

5) Write down five ideas you can use for direct-mail promotions.

3

When you reach for the stars, you may not quite get one, but you won't come up with a handful of mud, either.

—Leo Burnett

There's a Customer on Line Two

One of your greatest sources of new mobile DJ business is sitting right there on your desk. It's your telephone. Every time your phone rings, you should hear a cash register ringing in your head. Remember, every call is an opportunity for you to book another gig.

A ringing telephone can also be an opportunity for you to alienate prospects and ensure that they'll never book you. Every time you answer the telephone, your company's image is on the line. And you never get a second chance to make a good first impression.

Think about how you and your employees answer your phone. Do customers feel glad they called you—or do they feel like they're intruding on your day? Do you come across as being friendly, courteous and professional? Or do you sound like you don't know, you don't care, and you don't want to be bothered?

What are your goals when you answer the phone? To answer questions? To give out prices? To get off the phone as quickly as possible? Do you try to find out who's calling? Do you ask for the caller's name, and try for an address and phone number? Do you try to get them to meet with you face-to-face?

Our company conducts "Telephone Opportunity" programs for high-ticket retail companies across the United States. These programs stress the importance of getting callers' names and phone numbers and setting appointments every time the phone rings. A major portion of the pro-

---

Your Phone Number Is Important

Customers feel most comfortable dealing with a DJ who is "local." You may think nothing of driving two hours to a gig, but many customers would not call you if they thought you were that far away from their event. That's why having a local phone number is so important. If you live outside of a major city, look into getting a telephone number with that city's exchange, then using call-forwarding to have all of your calls ring in at your home or office. People will feel more comfortable dialing a number with an exchange they recognize as being from their area.

You may also want to consider a vanity phone number, to make it easy for prospects to remember your number. Something like CALLADJ (225-5235) or 695-JAMS (695-5267) or MRMUSIC (676-8742). Choosing your own phone number will cost you a little more, but you may find that it's worth it for the increase in calls you receive.

gram involves secret-shopper-type calls to thousands of locations. No matter what the industry: mobile DJ, music, automobiles or air conditioners, the results are usually the same. Initial calls result in some 80 percent of the people answering the phone never even asking for the caller's name.

Let me tell you about a recent campaign. Many times, a phone would ring eight or 10 times before it was answered. That's annoying. But here's a new one: 25 percent of the time, we got electronic answering. You know... press 1 for this, 2 for that, etc. What we learned here was that it irritates a lot of people who want to talk to a human being as quickly as possible, particularly if they're not exactly sure what they want. Many callers today immediately press "0" because they think that will get a human on the phone. But it doesn't always work. And when "0" doesn't work or when a human doesn't come on the line in a reasonable amount of time, prospects might just hang up and call the next DJ in the Yellow Pages.

Twenty percent of the time we got an answering machine. The number was even higher when I called some DJs before the show in Las Vegas—65 percent of you have answering machines. This is not a bad thing. I know that you have other jobs and you can't be there. But the type of greeting you have on your machine can make all the difference.

We've found that callers are more apt to leave a message if the message on the machine isn't bland and uncaring. Maybe you have a machine that picks up after hours, or when all of the salespeople are busy. What's your current message? Is it: "We're not here to take your call right now, but if you leave your name, number and a brief message, we'll call you back as soon as possible?" If it is, you're the same as everybody else. Everybody has this message: the dry cleaner, the florist, the gas station, and the pharmacy. You probably have the same message on your machine at home.

You're in the entertainment business. Someone calling you is looking for an entertainer. Give them a taste of what you offer. Make your message more interesting than the others. If you're not entertaining, you're not going to increase your business by 30 percent starting next month, or next year, or ever!

When you answer the phone, the first five seconds give the caller a mental image of your company. Does the person answering the phone sing the last syllables of the name of your business like the feature song from a Broadway play? There's one company that we deal with on a regular basis whose name ends with the word "Enterprises." The receptionist says, "Good morning, Ajax Enter-prya-zzzzehhzz." You get tired just waiting for her to finish the word. Another company we call regularly has a receptionist who answers the phone like she's having a sexual experience. She's so breathy that some people actually go there to see what she looks like.

What image does your company portray? When you go to lunch today, call your business. Pretend you're a customer. Does the person on the phone sound soft, sad and morbid as if you're calling a funeral home? Or does he or she sound bright and cheerful and really glad you called?

Everyone who answers the phone should make an all-out effort to sound nice and use some personality. The whole idea here is that incoming calls are your best source of leads and new business. Don't take them for granted. If you capitalize on every single one, your mobile DJ business could increase substantially in just a very short time, without increasing your costs one bit.

First You Need to Find Out Who's Calling

Write or type the word "OPPORTUNITY" on a small piece of paper and tape it to your phone. That will remind you and your employees that you have a great opportunity to make a sale or create a new customer every time you pick up the phone.

Always make sure you ask for a name, try for a phone number (or an address for your mailing list) and try to set an appointment to meet with the caller if you can't book them right on the phone.

Getting the caller's name should be one of the first things you do when you pick up the phone. Getting a name shows that you care about the caller. If you get their names right away, you can use them throughout the conversation. Everybody loves the sound of their own name. The easiest way to get the prospect's name is to offer yours when you answer the phone, then ask for the caller's.

Use your first and last name when answering the phone. The prospect will normally answer with his or her full name if you say:

"This is (your name). Who am I speaking to?" After they respond, continue with, "Nice to talk to you, (prospect's name). How can I help you?"

Unless prospects offer only their first names, call them by their surnames, i.e., Mr. Jones or Mrs. Smith—it shows professional respect.

Getting the prospect's phone number is just as important as getting his or her name. Without a phone number, you have no way of assuring that you'll ever talk to this prospect again. And you can't rely on the phone book—most list dozens of Smiths, Jones and Browns, along with numerous spelling variations.

Give a valid reason for wanting a phone number. If the prospect asks you a question that you can't answer right away, say you'll look into it and call back—of course, you'll need the phone number to do that.

If the prospect resists giving you his number, assure him that you won't call without a very good reason. Then find one and follow up!

Phone Tips

Tell everyone to ask for callers' names and phone numbers and try to get the callers to make an appointment for a face-to-face meeting if they can't be booked over the phone. Here are some tips to keep in mind every time the phone rings:

- Make up some fact sheets to keep by the telephone with a pen. Include spaces for all of the information you should get every time a prospect calls: name, address, phone number, date and time of the event, length of the event, type of event, location of the event, price quoted, extras, age group, date of a face-to-face appointment, etc.
- Help the prospect feel comfortable speaking with you. Treat each call like it's the most important one you've ever taken.
- Show a sincere interest in helping the prospect with his or her event.
- Smile when you introduce yourself. The prospect will hear the smile in your voice.

Take advantage of every telephone opportunity. Each call is a potential new customer, current client, or sale. Treat them like gold. They're worth it.

You should also try to get callers' addresses. With an address, prospects can be included in future mailings. If they don't book you right away, future mailings will keep you in their thoughts. You can also keep in touch by sending them an occasional note.

Ask callers if they'd like you to send them information on the packages you've discussed during your conversation. Here's an example: "I'd like to send you a brochure that explains our party packages in detail. Let me have your address and I'll get it out in tonight's mail." Telephone prospects are more likely to share information with you if you show them a benefit first.

If the caller doesn't book you during your conversation, send out the brochure you mentioned as soon as you hang up the phone. But don't leave it at that. Include a music list and an agreement all made out except their signature. Make it easy for them to buy! If they liked you on the telephone, like what your brochure has to say, and are impressed by your music list, they may just send back a signed contract. (By the way, don't include the line "Does the DJ get to eat?" on the contract. That's tacky.)

Try to establish some rapport with callers. Get them to like you. People are more apt to buy from someone they like.

On the phone, your voice is the only impression callers have of you and your business. They may not be aware of your extensive play list, service or dedication. Setting an appointment gives you the chance to meet your callers face-to-face, and it gives them the opportunity to see what a great mobile DJ operation you have.

Meeting with customers is always a good idea, even if they do book you right over the phone. It gives you more of a taste of their personalities so you know which of your DJs would fit best for their events. If you are going to handle the gig yourself, it's nice to at least know what the person who hired you looks like when you arrive at the event. And meeting with prospects and customers ahead of time reassures them of your professionalism. If you have an office, it's easy for prospects or customers to come in and listen to and choose some music for special parts of their events (bride's first dance, CEO's announcement, etc.).

When the Customer Asks the Price Over the Phone

When somebody calls us on the phone, they're calling for two reasons. Number one, to do some business with us, and number two, to eliminate us from consideration. Of course, we have a few objectives of our own. Our objectives are to find out who's calling, get their phone numbers or addresses, and then book them.

In a recent survey, 5,000 businesses were called across the country. The only question asked was: "How much is your product?" or "How much is your service?" The results were amazing:

- 11 percent said they didn't know, that they weren't the right person to ask, and that the caller should call back later.

  People aren't going to call you back later! They're going to call the next DJ listed in the Yellow Pages. And if the person answering the phone at the other DJ business knows what he or she is doing, then that DJ is going to get the sale.

- 34 percent gave the price, then hung up without any further conversation.

  Maybe they were busy. Maybe they were having a bad day and didn't want to be bothered. Or maybe they just didn't know any better.

- 48 percent gave the price and told the caller about other products or services they offered, but didn't try for a sale, an appointment or any other type of action.

  Maybe they didn't want to seem pushy. Maybe they figured if someone wanted to buy something from them, they'd ask.

Maybe they didn't want to make too much money and get moved into a higher tax bracket by the IRS.

- 45 percent let the phone ring for more than 45 seconds—eight times—before they answered it.

  Not many customers will wait that long for you to answer your phone. If you're too busy to help them, maybe your competitors can find time.

- 78 percent never asked for the caller's name!

  All they knew was that somebody called and said they wanted to spend a lot of money, and that maybe they'd stop in some time or call back. The people answering the phone never asked for a name. They didn't try to get the caller to make an appointment. Do you believe it?! Well, it happens all the time. Don't let it happen to you.

You spend money on advertising, you spend money on your Yellow Pages listing, and you've got substantial daily overhead. You have a big investment in your business, and when the phone rings, the person who answers it is in full control of your operation. He or she is often the deciding factor in whether callers decide to book you or go elsewhere.

Here's a suggestion for you. Don't quote prices within the first 30 seconds of a phone call. When prospects ask "How much," you can say something like, "We have a range of packages available."

You can't really give an accurate quote without some more information, so ask, "Let's get an idea of what you're looking for." Then ask questions about the size of the event, where it's going to be held, how long you'll be there, how far you'll have to travel, and so forth.

Then work on getting the caller to like you. Don't rattle off the big figures right away. Because if you do, you're likely to hear a click and a dial tone as the caller moves on to the next DJ in the Yellow Pages. If they insist on getting a price right away, give them a range. Say something like, "Well, the price ranges from $XXX to $XXX. Let's see what package will be best for your event."

You spend all this money on business cards, brochures, advertising, equipment, music and so on ... don't blow it when it comes to talking to people on the phone. When someone calls, the first thing you have to do is get that person to like you. If people like you, they will trust you, and if they trust you, they will book you.

It's also important to let the customer do most of the talking. You do the listening. They will tell you what it's going to take to have you be their DJ. You have two ears and one mouth: use them in that proportion. In other words, if you do most of the talking, you probably won't get the gig. If they do most of the talking, they will talk themselves into buying your service. It's really that easy. You have to be their friend, and you have to ask lots of questions, but you really have to listen to their answers, too.

Everyone loves to talk about themselves. I'll probably pay more if you get me to be your friend, and you tell me what a great job you're going to do for me. Ask me what DJs I've used in the past. Ask what I paid. Make conversation.

There was a survey done by the University of Southern California on what basis people use to form opinions and perceptions about others. The survey found that only 7 percent of people's perceptions is based on the words others say. Another 38 percent is based on how we sound when we say the words, and 55 percent is based on visual cues.

Guess what? On the phone, nobody can see you. So to be really effective, that 7 percent from words becomes really important. Use words a 12-year-old could understand. Don't talk over your customers' heads. Don't use DJ jargon or jive.

The survey found that people are more believable when they speak slowly and with a lower tone of voice. Think about how you would feel, for example, if you were flying from Chicago to Las Vegas, and the pilot came on the intercom sounding like Edith Bunker from *All in the Family*. I bet that you wouldn't feel as secure as you would if the pilot talked more like Walter Cronkite.

I like to hear phrases like: "No problem. We do it a lot. We can take care of that for you." These are the things your prospects want to hear. They can't see you. Make your words count.

Questions & Thought-Starters

1) What three things should everyone answering the phone try to get from callers? Why are these things important?

2) Check your answering machine message. How does it sound? How could you improve it?

3) What could you do to make it easier and more convenient for customers to reach you by telephone?

4) What is the easiest way to get a caller's name? Phone number? To set an appointment?

5) Write down some things you can say the next time someone calls and asks you for a price right away.

 *Opportunity is missed by most people because it is dressed in overalls and looks like work.*

—*Thomas Edison*

A Different Look at Shows

I love consumer events: home shows, auto shows, electronic shows, boat shows, you name it. I especially love to go during cold winter months when there isn't a whole lot else going on. Actually, I've never bought much at a show. I've spent a lot of time looking around. The usual routine is to get a shopping bag or two, fill them up with about 15 pounds of brochures and literature, add 20 or 30 business cards, talk to anyone who wants to make conversation, and forget about them entirely after I get home. Great fun. Makes for a heck of a day.

My neighbor's oldest daughter got married a couple of months ago. I knew they had gone to a couple of bridal shows, so I asked them if that's where they chose their DJ, florist, and other vendors. She said, "No, the bridal shows certainly told me who *not* to deal with." She said that she left her name at one display with a DJ who never got back to her. Another DJ was way too expensive. Another one was rude. "When you're really ready to make a decision, give me a call," was all he said.

Think about your displays at mall shows, bridal shows, or any type of consumer event. Are you in category A: "What can we do to talk to a lot of people?" or category B: "How long before we can get the heck out of here?" Be honest. Standing on your feet for 12 straight hours can be a little bit of a strain, particularly if you're not selling anything. But when you're booking dates and setting appointments to follow up with a lot of potential clients, time can go very quickly.

The key to successful consumer events is attitude. If you have the right attitude, the right selling skills, and the right display, you can do a lot of business.

Not only can you increase business from these exposures on a very limited budget, by using a separate table for a free drawing, you can also produce a great mailing list of semi-qualified leads. The secret here is to have the free drawing table staffed, and the free-drawing cards should qualify the registrants. Find out the date of their wedding, next corporate party, or whatever type of event they're planning. Give away something of value that will appeal to the largest number of people walking by. Your entry cards will qualify them so you can determine which people are qualified prospects.

Work through the cards immediately after the show. Follow up with qualified prospects within a week. When you give away the grand prize from your drawing, take a picture of the winner and send it to the local newspaper as a news item.

Bridal shows and other consumer events can be great opportunities for building business. They increase exposure and media attention, and they can help you expand your mailing list for future events, as well.

There are two things to remember when planning a promotion at a bridal show or other consumer event. First of all, no matter how great your display is, your selling skills have to be really sharp. You usually don't get a second chance at a customer—at least not at the show. You have to close quickly and often. Talk to everybody. Ask them to book as soon as you perceive the first degree of acceptance. Make it easy to buy. Offer a gift coupon for a free light show or some other benefit to people who book at the show. Have a definite plan of attack, and have a reason ready for a customer to book you now.

Second, selling at this type of exposure is a numbers game. The more people you ask to buy, the more bookings you'll make. If you don't ask, you don't get.

Attracting Buyers to Your Display

If you can't find someone to talk to, you're not going to sell anything to anybody. Any way you can get a potential prospect to stop is important. Don't just set up your display and hope people will flock to it. That doesn't happen. You must have the right point-of-sale cards, the right look, and the right attitude.

The location of your booth is very important. The best sales locations are near a main entrance. This way you get prospects when they're still fresh, unhurried, and willing to talk. Choose a spot that is surrounded by as many aisles as possible. This will funnel more traffic to your display. Make sure that your identification is visible from all directions. Avoid drafty or cold spots, areas near eating spots, any smoking areas, and poorly lit corners.

One way to get more exposure at a show is by offering your services to the show's organizers. For example, at a bridal show, you may be able to trade providing your services during the fashion show for an ad in the show guide, a bigger booth, or additional signage. You'll also gain credibility from being associated with the organizers.

People like to do business where business is being done. Make it look like you're busy even if nothing is going on. Don't sit down. Keep looking for someone to talk to. Keep a smile on your face. Outside shows are supposed to be fun. A bad attitude will make you look bad. Don't get involved with lengthy personal discussions with any staff you might have in your booth or someone at a neighboring booth.

Remember why you're there: to get more bookings. In order to sell something, you've got to get people to stop. Here are some of the basics for finding people to talk to at a consumer event.

Point-of-Sale Cards: Every display should have one or more point-of-sale cards citing reasons to book—on the spot. The cards should be different sizes, all of the same style and color. Don't use carelessly cut cardboard and sloppy printing. Have professional-quality signs.

Be clever when coming up with ideas for your point-of-sale cards. See what other people use in their booths. Think of what would get your attention. What would it take to get you to stop?

Equipment Does Not Sell. People coming to a typical consumer event don't know the difference between different brands of equipment. Nor do they know (or will they be impressed by) how much it costs. Show some of your equipment, but don't rely on it to attract people to your booth. It won't.

Have a Brochure Printed Specifically for the Show: It doesn't cost a lot of money to have a flier or folder printed up that says *Show Special Edition* or something that lists the bargains and advantages of your DJ service. Printed materials make your claims of special prices and unique opportunities more believable. Make sure your handout contains a lot of pictures and clearly lists the packages you have available, a sample of your playlist, and your phone number. Explain plenty of reasons why shoppers should book you right away.

The idea is not just to have bunches of brochures lying on top of your equipment. Hold them in your hand, giving them out to people you talk to. It's a great way to start a conversation. People like things that are free. You might even consider printing a price on it, like a special show publication. Then when you hand one out, it will seem like more than just an ordinary giveaway.

What Happens When People Do Stop?

When people do stop by, give them a few seconds to feel comfortable at your display. Then get into a conversation with them. Opening lines are important. Don't say, "Can I help you?" Come up with something different, something that can't be answered by just a "yes" or a "no." For example:

- "What brings you to the show today?"
- "What type of music do you like?"

Or you might start a conversation with opening lines that have a one-word answer which can lead to further conversation:

- "Have you thought about hiring a DJ for your next party?"
- "Are you looking for a great entertainer for your next corporate event?"
- "Do you like Latin music?"

You get the idea. Ignoring people who stop is the worst thing you can do. Talk to everyone at your display. You have to keep up this routine. The more people you talk to, the better your chances of closing a sale. It's as simple as that. Many sales have been made starting with, "Where are you folks from?"

Talk to everybody, every person who stops or slows down. Even talk to the people who work at the show. Everyone is a prospect. Don't wait for people to come in the booth or display with their checkbooks open. It doesn't happen that often.

Using Freebies

Everybody loves to get something for free. Giving something away is a great way to get people to stop at your booth. But as you know, many people who go to consumer shows like to see how many things they can take home for free. They go around with plastic bags and almost expect you to drop in a pen, key chain or whatever. It's like an adult version of trick-or-treat. So the effectiveness of your giveaway depends on how you use it.

I remember a gentleman named Maury Lindenfeld who used to set up a display at home shows, sport shows and mall shows. Maury would have dozens of ball point pens all nicely positioned

Some Important Things to Remember:

Do ask everyone to book you at the show.

Do maintain a professional attitude.

Do take pride in your appearance and manners.

Do set a goal for yourself on a daily basis.

Do keep a smile on your face.

Don't show up late and leave early.

Don't talk so loudly that other customers can hear your sales pitch.

Don't play loud music. Keep it soft and generic.

Don't look poorly dressed.

Don't promise a customer anything that is based upon "guesswork." Stick to the facts.

Don't let the display get dirty.

Don't eat or smoke in your display.

in the back of his booth, and as you passed by, he'd have a couple in his hand. If you expressed interest in his product or just a pen, he'd hand you the pen. But when he handed it to you, he'd pull the cap off and keep it in his hand. Then he'd start talking like crazy to find out your name, whether you were a potential customer, and where you lived. You'd stand there with half a pen in your hand waiting for old Maury to release the other part. And he got your attention for awhile.

Less effective was a DJ I remember who would put up a display at local county fairs. He'd give away a miniature CD key chain imprinted with his store name to anybody who stopped by. He figured that if he gave away a thousand key chains, he'd had a good show. Never mind if he got any bookings or not.

The idea here isn't to just give stuff away! It's a means to an end. You give things away to get people to stop. When they stop, you try to get them to book.

Some DJs use advertising specialties to bring in more bookings week after week, while others have a tough time just paying for them at the end of the month. It's not what you have imprinted, it's how you use it. You have to have a game plan on how these things are going to bring you more business.

The appeal of freebies lies in the very human need to feel that one is coming out ahead. Everyone likes to get something for free. It's a great concept. Use it to your best advantage.

Questions & Thought-Starters

1) Make a sketch of the cards you'll use for a free drawing at your next consumer event. What information will you need to get from prospects?

2) How can you maximize the exposure you get at a consumer event?

3) Make a sketch of how you'd like to set up your booth at the next consumer event you participate in. Where will you put equipment, point-of-sale cards, etc.?

4) Come up with some more opening lines to use to start a conversation with prospects at consumer events.

5) What freebies could you use effectively at the next consumer event you work?

5 *There is only one boss. The customer. And he can fire anybody in the company from the chairman on down, simply by spending his money somewhere else.*

—Sam Walton

What Ever Happened to ... ?

The last "Cheers" episode has come and gone, but with cable television bringing in 50 channels or more to households all over the country, there always seems to be a rerun of "Cheers" on somewhere.

Did you ever listen to the words of the "Cheers" theme? It says people want to go "where everybody knows your name and they're always glad you came." People like to go where they feel they are known. Customers like to do business with people who take a personal interest in them.

It's true in the mobile DJ business as well. Have you ever played the game "What ever happened to... (a certain customer)?"

I bet if you sat down and worked at it, you could come up with an easy dozen names of regular customers who no longer call.

Why?

Sure, you probably won't perform more than one wedding gig for a person (of course, you can never tell) but other family members may be getting married. And if you impress one corporate planner or someone who books a lot of DJs for local events, that person could become a valuable repeat customer.

You'll be interested in a survey done by a nationally known organization that chose at random a list of 100 retail customers who had not made a purchase or a visit to the same store within a year or two. They sent out 100 questionnaires, followed through, and came up with these results:

- 68 customers had no special reason for staying away ... they just never came in again.
- 14 had complaints that were not taken care of properly.
- Nine were lured away by other stores (better service or lower prices).
- Nine moved or died.

In other words, nearly seven out of 10 good customers left because the store let them leave. Are you making the same mistakes in your DJ business?

You plan and work on your ads, do outside events, and come up with promotions and direct mailers to get your phone ringing. What are you doing to keep customers coming back or at least referring you?

The typical mobile DJ often feels boxed in by too much work. How can you possibly put together an ongoing clever direct-mail campaign, when you are involved with the day-to-day running of a business, worrying about employees, handling bookings, making payroll, and sweating out the financial problem of the day?

Who has the time?

Let's think about this logically. Where is your best source of more business? It's previous customers.

Retailer Murray Raphel likens selling to cranking up an airplane engine. Turning over an engine by hand is a difficult procedure. But once you have spun the prop, the engine is running and begins to spin on its own.

How do you get your customers to call you again? How do you get them to refer other customers to you?

It takes a personal touch. And a personal relationship with your customers is your strongest selling tool. People go miles out of their way for "service." Distance can be secondary when getting a haircut, buying shoes, going to the dentist, or looking for advice on landscaping. Customers will go where people take a personal interest and know them when they walk in.

And guess what. Price will be secondary if people think that you're their friend. It makes it easier to get your standard rate for a four-hour party, even if a competitor is offering a special. When customers feel you have their best interests at heart, it's less likely they'll want to shop other DJs looking for a lower price. Nothing will help increase your profit margin more than customers booking without quibbling over price. When you're their friend, sometimes those sales come a lot easier.

Do you think Cliff and Norm sit at Cheers because draft beer is a nickel cheaper? Like the "Cheers" song says, you go where your friends are... "and everybody knows your name."

If you don't have a database of previous (and current) customers, now is the time to start one. Repeat business starts with contacting every previous customer several times a year. Don't let them slip over to your competition.

Invite past and present customers to participate in open houses and to take advantage of seasonal offers. Get them to call or meet with you to see what's new.

Follow up your direct mail with an occasional phone call. I know, I know. It takes time. Who has time to come up with a direct-mail piece, stuff and seal the envelopes, stick on the stamps and take them to the post office?

I even hate bringing up the "calling old customers on the phone" routine to find out if you can get them to book or refer you one more time. That could really ruin a long lunch hour. It's always easier just to see if somebody new will call.

Constant customer contact is an important thing. Keeping in touch with your old customers will ensure that they will call and book you again (and refer their friends, too).

People like to go where everybody knows their name.

So... before you wonder "What ever happened to old 'what's-her-name'" again, ask yourself what you have done lately to make her want to come back. Do you keep in touch with your customers on a regular basis, or do you just let them ride out into the sunset on their own?

Questions & Thought-Starters

1) Take 10 minutes to make a list of some regular customers who haven't booked you in awhile. Why did they stop calling? (In Chapter 7, you'll learn some techniques to bring them back.)

2) Now write down three things you can do to keep more customers off of that list.

3) What is your strongest selling tool?

4) Why are personal relationships so important in selling?

5) Why do you need to stay in contact with your customers?

You miss 100 percent of the shots you never take.

—Wayne Gretzky

Turning Leads into Sales

In the mobile DJ business, bookings are what determine how much money you're going to make. Obviously the more bookings you make, the more money you'll gross at the end of each month.

Waiting for the next person to call is no guarantee that you're going to book a gig. It's a lot easier to sell to someone you already know and who knows you. Actively pursuing a prospect and lead list gives you customers to talk to day after day, week after week, and month after month.

That's where good lead follow-up comes in. It's relationship marketing. It's turning the people on your prospect and lead list into long-term customers. This is where following up a lead really counts. Don't confuse the function of your job with your goal. Your *goal* is to book more gigs. Your *function* is to create and maintain customers.

Think of all the places you can access to find names, prospects and potential customers... without having to rely on strangers. Your newspaper, Yellow Pages, and radio ads create leads. And then you have referrals from current and past customers, leads from bridal shows, mall displays, etc. It all adds up to a lot of names. These leads can bring you a ton of new business, if you follow them up in a conscientious manner.

It's also important to remember that leads are perishable. They have to be followed up quickly. Leads can cool down fast. A hot lead today may be no lead tomorrow.

Lead follow-up is nothing more than making contact, staying in touch and trying to get the person to meet with you for the first or one more time. A creative, effective lead follow-up program is a necessity if you want to increase your income substantially. Sometimes we have to really push ourselves to do it. Sometimes it's the last thing we want to do each day. And sometimes getting started isn't easy.

Have a Plan and a Goal

Lead follow-up does not mean sweating it out hour after hour on the phone. A few minutes a day is all it takes.

Effective lead follow-up is simply letting interested prospects know who you are, what you do, and where you do it. You also want them to know you're a pretty nice person to deal with.

Think about this. Would you rather buy from a stranger or from a friend? Would you rather deal with someone you know or someone you don't know?

The answer is pretty obvious. People like to be known. They like recognition and they like to deal with friends. It's tough to get a booking from someone who doesn't know you, doesn't like you or doesn't trust you. The first step in following up leads is getting the prospects to like you. If they like you, they're more apt to trust you. And if they trust you, it's easier to get them to buy.

This is not hard. Follow-up is just the continuing process of staying in touch with prospects until you book them. Wanting to do it is not enough. Knowing how to do it is the most important part.

First you need a system. It should be one that you're comfortable with, whether that's a 3" x 5" card file or a computer program you like. Remem-

Numbers You Should Know

On a national average, only 20 percent of all leads that are generated are ever followed-up. That means that 80 percent of all leads are never contacted. However, 78 percent of people who show an interest end up buying what they were looking for somewhere—with a good follow-up system they could be doing business with you.

ber, it's the information that goes into the system that's important.

Keep track of everything you learn about your prospects so you can talk intelligently with them when you call. Don't just write down information relating to the possible job, also make note of their personal interests and hobbies, so you can refer to them in future contacts. This way you can talk to prospects about something other than the gig. You'll seem more like a friend than a salesperson if you say, "How did you do at your club's golf tournament last week?" Take good notes on your lead cards and keep your system updated and organized.

Follow Up Regularly

- 90 percent of all leads who are contacted once and don't make a purchase, are never contacted again.

- 82 percent who don't make a purchase can't even remember the name of the salesperson a year later.

- 62 percent of the people who hire you have a friend or relative who may be looking for a DJ in the next year as well.

If you use your system correctly, you'll know exactly where you stand on booking a gig with a particular prospect. Remember: the best systems are the ones that are used consistently.

You can't give leads lip-service. You can't just send a letter or a gift to a recent customer and call that a follow-up program. And you can't send out a preprinted form letter or postcard commemorating a holiday once in a while thinking you're doing a great job. It takes a combination of phone contact and direct mail *with a personal touch* to keep prospects coming in to see you on a regular basis.

Using the Phone

The greatest source of new leads and more business is your telephone. The best way to capitalize on this sales opportunity is to take advantage of every call.

Your phone is also the easiest tool to use for follow-up. It's right there in front of you every day. One of the secrets to following up leads on the phone is to not make too many calls at once. Don't take a stack of 30 people you want to contact, only to get started and get burned out after the fifth call. Pace yourself. Follow up leads in small doses.

Telephone follow-up is not calling strangers and trying to sell them on your DJ services. It is establishing rapport and setting a pattern for constant contact.

Each time you call your prospect, make sure it's with a legitimate reason. Each call must have a purpose. *Don't* start a phone conversation by saying something like: "Have you made a decision yet?"

It's easier if you pick up the phone and say something like this: "I was thinking about your wedding plans when I was driving to work this morning and I thought of something that will solve some of your age-mix problems."

You see, when you call a prospect one more time, you should never call to get something. Always call to give something. You can call to give more information or to offer a brochure.

Every Prospect Is Different

No two prospects are alike. What works with one person might not work with the next. Be creative and follow them up in the manner best suited to each individual.

Sometimes humor works when used appropriately and with the right people. A laugh is a great way to lighten the mood of a conversation. A bit of personality can go a long way.

The way you end the conversation with your prospect is also important. It can make or break your follow-up. If you're searching for things to say to your prospect, the call will surely end on an awkward note. It's much easier and more effective to end a conversation that involves sending out print material by suggesting a time for you to call once they have received the information. It gives you a legitimate reason for calling and gives you something to talk about when you do call again. Remember, the whole idea is to get to know them and be a friend.

Following Up Leads with Direct Mail

When following up your leads using direct mail, you want to make a good impression. Your cards and notes should have a personal touch showing that you care about your prospects as individuals.

The most important thing to remember when using direct mail is to remind your prospects of who you are. If you write your notes by hand, they should be neat and legible. Make the notes very personal. Use the word "I" not "we." For example: "*I* want to meet you, *I* want to earn your business." Show them that you're sincere and always ready to help them with their event plans.

If you use preprinted postcards or form letters, take it upon yourself to at least add a handwritten P.S. at the bottom. It could be something of a personal nature relating to previous conversations, like: "Hope your son's doing well in Little League." A personal note shows that you care and that this person is important to you.

Think about it this way. How many Christmas cards do you receive that are preprinted? They just say "The Jones Family" or "Bill and Ethel Smith." You know they bought those cards by the dozen and are slipping them into envelopes as quickly as they can. Now, how much more special does it make you feel if you get such a card with a note written in pen: "Hi John and Mary, hope we can get together over the holidays"? Make prospects feel special if you want them to think of you as more than a salesperson.

Here's an idea for following up a lead by phone and mail. If you've been talking to someone over the phone, but they haven't returned your calls for a while, try sending them a postcard. Just write, "Dear Mrs. Jones, I have good news for you! Give me a call," and sign your name.

Everybody loves good news. Maybe your news is that you have another availability. Maybe you have some new equipment or a new routine.

You can use the same technique when you're following up leads by phone and get an answering machine. What usually happens is you blurt out a bunch of information, and the person you're calling never returns your call. The next time you get an answering machine, try leaving the message "I have good news for you," with your name and phone number.

Mailing Lists

Keep your prospects and leads on your mailing list forever. Even if they're not in the market now to hire a mobile DJ, they could be in the future. Get in the habit of constantly updating your list.

Be sure to replace current addresses with new ones once you get them. Your lead list is your most valuable tool when using direct mail. But you need to keep it current to get the best possible use from it.

Repetition is the key to using direct mail effectively. Sending your prospects one card once is not going to make a sale for you. They need to be reminded often of who you are.

Other Ideas

Any time you set an appointment, follow it up with a thank-you/reminder card. This will add a personal touch and help prospects remember the appointment.

Sending your business card along in the mail gives your prospects easy access to your name and phone number. Having your picture on the card will help customers visualize a real person instead of just a voice on the other end of the phone.

Become the only mobile DJ your prospects know. Get them to think of you as soon as they're ready to book.

People Who Book the Competition

You can't book every gig. Not every lead you follow up is going to choose you for one reason or another. But they're still important people for you. Don't take them off of your mailing list. Don't take them out of your database.

Send them a note. Say you enjoyed meeting them. Whatever event they booked with your competition is probably not the last event they're ever going to be involved with. They may have hired a competitor for their class reunion, but maybe they'll choose you for their son's bar mitzvah. In the meantime, if they liked you well enough, they will probably recommend you to their friends. Even if people don't book you, they can still be a valuable source of referrals and leads.

Sending Notes and Letters

The best method to use when following up a new lead is usually a phone call followed by mail. When you call, you can say you'll be sending mail.

Here are a few rules for best results:
- Type it or have someone type it for you. If you write it by hand, use a black felt-tip pen.
- Have someone proofread everything for spelling or grammatical errors.
- Neatness and legibility do count.
- Every note should have a personal touch.

No matter what the situation, whether you're talking to a prospect for the first time on the telephone or when they've already booked someone else, never bad-mouth the competition. It just makes you look bad. Focus instead on what you have to offer. Highlight the fact that you always send two people, a DJ and an MC, to every wedding, or that you guarantee you'll have every request. Never stoop to name-calling. That's for children. You're a professional.

Follow-Up Does Work

You can't guess who your next buyers will be. Keep in touch with everyone on your lead and prospect lists until they buy or die. Following up your leads is the most important part of increasing your bookings.

All of the mobile DJs who make a lot of money have a good lead follow-up program and all of the mobile DJs who have good a lead follow-up program make a lot of money. The next step is up to you. With a well-thought out plan and lead follow-up program that is used consistently, you're well on your way to increasing your mobile DJ sales by 30 percent or more, right away.

Questions & Thought-Starters

1) Which is easier: waiting for new customers or selling your services to someone who already knows you? Which is more effective? Which do you spend most of your time doing?

2) List five places where you can find new prospects' names.

3) What kind of lead follow-up system do you use now? How well does it work for you? Could you improve it?

4) Why is it important to have at least a small handwritten message on direct-mail follow-up pieces?

5) Why should you follow-up with people who booked a competitor?

6) When should you take a person off of your follow-up list?

7

More sales are made with friendship than with salesmanship.

—*Jeffrey H. Gitomer*

Bringing Them Back Alive

Good leads can be no leads at all if you can't get them in while they are still hot about booking a DJ. Hot leads can turn cold fast. You can't wait a week or a month before contacting people who show interest. And each time you contact them, you want to make sure their interest level is still high.

However you track your leads, whether you're using a prospect card system, or if you've got them on a computer, you can grade them on a scale of 1 to 10 each time you talk to them. Write down how hot are they at the time. Prospects get a "1" rating when they are not even lukewarm, have very little interest, and would like you to stop bothering them ... they'll call you when they're ready. Those earning a 10 are red-hot, ready-to-go, and ready-to-sign on the dotted line. Where do your prospects stand at the time you're talking with them? Write it down. Put it on their prospect cards. Each time you talk with them, try to get that level up a notch.

It's one thing to try to arrange another appointment. But it's another thing altogether to get them in as a level seven or eight, rather than a two or three. Let them picture how happy they will be at their special event with you spinning the discs. Find out where the prospect's hot-button is. Is it variety of music? Price versus quality? Special effects? Keeping up with and outdoing the Joneses? Interactive MCs and dancers?

Take the instance of a young couple in Jacksonville, Florida who were planning their wedding. They called around and made an appointment with a DJ who was highly recommended by a few different people. They were really

---

Some Self-analysis

- Do you expect some price resistance when quoting for a gig?
- Do you try to determine a customer's excitement level?
- Do you work at trying to be as excited as well?
- Do you try to paint a mental picture of how the gig will go in your customers' minds?
- Do you try to use the phrases: "It's easy."

    "What can we do to really make you happy?"

    "We want to earn your business."

    "We've done this many times and have many excited, happy customers... and we want you to feel the same."

excited about having a lot of special effects and group activities at their reception, but unfortunately the DJ didn't share their enthusiasm. Instead of hearing how happy they would be with the DJ's services, they heard these exact phrases:

- "We're really booked up at that time of the year. Do you really need that much lighting?"
- "We don't do much in the way of audience participation."
- "Lighting, fog machines, and other special effects all cost extra, you know."
- "Are you sure you want confetti guns?"
- "Of course this is the best we can do price-wise ... we're professionals."
- "Are you sure you can afford it?"

This is a true story. Guess who they didn't hire. Instead, they called a DJ recommended by another friend. This (smarter) DJ said:

- "No problem."
- "What will it take to make you happy?"
- "How many strobes do we have? Well, how many do you want?"
- "We'll handle everything."

This DJ found their hot button: It wasn't price. It was fun! They had a lot of money from her parents and wanted to go all out at their wedding. They really wanted to deal with someone who would make their reception one big party.

Remember to keep your comments positive when talking to prospects. Sometimes we tend to paint a picture without even knowing that we are doing so. Choose your words and phrases carefully. And retain and keep raising that level of excitement your customer already has.

You have to put some effort and enthusiasm into your job if you want people to keep booking you. Make customers feel like you're just as excited about their event as they are. Help them develop confidence in you.

Don't Forget to Say "Thank You"

You always want to give prospects and customers reasons to book you one more time. You want them to trust you and feel comfortable. Take a lesson from my tailor. When I opened up my mail the other day, I found a handwritten note from a men's shop where I had recently purchased a new suit. It was from the gentleman who sold me the suit, telling me how much he really appreciated my business and hoped I would come back again. I was surprised to get it, because the men's shop was very small, and not only did this person sell me the suit, he tailored it personally as well. Not only that, he spoke only broken English and did not have what we'd call "great literary skills." The note ended with: "Since this is how I earn my living, I want to make sure you are very happy. Maybe you will tell other people about my shop and I can make them happy, too. I want to earn your business. Thank you very much." *Business* was spelled wrong.

I got to thinking about the note. Among the things I recall buying in the last few months are a new car, carpeting for my home, some furniture and the new suit. For the office, we've purchased three new desks, eight new chairs for our conference room, two new VCRs, some recording equipment, plus some new computer equipment. Nobody else sent me a thank-you note. Nobody called to see if I was happy. Nobody said, "I want to earn your business." Sears didn't. JCPenney didn't. Office Max didn't. Radio Shack and Circuit City didn't. But Tony the tailor did. Tony's men's shop is in a little town of 30,000 people. It's 28 miles from my office.

I remembered that on the receipt for the suit, Tony had written "Thank you!" and signed his name. I guess he felt one "thank you" wasn't enough. He had to follow it up with a note as well. Since he probably can't spend a thousand dollars a month on newspaper advertising, or big bucks in the Yellow Pages, and has no TV or radio budget, he has to rely on referrals and current customers. Does it work? He said he wanted to "earn my business." He referred to me as his friend. I don't even remember how much the suit was, but I know I'll go back there for the next one.

Now here's where the story gets better. Last week, he called me and told me he got a new assortment of men's shirts in, with some very unique colors and styles. He had one that would go great with my suit, and would I like him to send it over to me UPS? Of course. No problem. Send it right away. Did I ever ask "how much?" Nope. I forgot to. It never occurred to me.

Do you send thank-you notes to your customers? Do you write "Thank You!" on the invoices and sign your name? Do you even have the time? Probably not. There are other things to do than have to write thank-you notes to people you've already worked for. They're already customers. You said "thank you" when you took their checks. If we're going to write to people, we usually first think to contact our current customers with sale fliers, statements, new product information, and regular customer mailings. But a note just to say thank you? C'mon. Wal-Mart doesn't. Price Club doesn't. And there's the point.

You want to be different than your competitors. Find different ways to appeal to your customers, to present your DJ services, and to develop and sustain customer interest. You want to be unique and interesting. Nothing is easier to ignore faster than a boring business.

Keeping customers coming back is the key to a successful mobile DJ business. Friends like to buy from friends. They buy from people they trust. If people like and trust you and your staff, price often becomes secondary. That human element of sincerity and appreciation is tough to compete with. It's a great way not only to increase your business, but to increase your profit margins as well.

So, think about it. Maybe it's time to start sending thank-you notes. What if 40 percent of those customers you thank booked you again, and referred you to their friends as well? Maybe you'd have to hire more DJs. It's worth a try.

Questions & Thought-Starters

1) How quickly should you follow up a lead? Why?

2) List some phrases that prospects want to hear you say.

3) Why is it important to thank your customers?

4) Think about some ways you can let your regular customers know that you really appreciate their business.

Even if you're on the right track—you're apt to get run over if you just stand there.

—Mark Twain

Basic Creative Sales Skills Are a Necessity

When my youngest daughter was home from college this summer, she decided to sell her old bike in a garage sale and buy a new mountain bike. I told her I'd go with her, and if she didn't have enough money saved up, I'd give her what she needed. There were only two stipulations:

1) It had to be a good-quality bike.
2) The salesperson had to ask us to buy it.

Now, I know there are a lot of good bicycles on the market. But what I didn't realize is that there are not many bicycle salespeople who ask customers to buy them.

I don't care how the salesperson asks. Anything would be acceptable. For example, I could handle:

"Wanna get it?" "Would you like it?" "OK with you?" "Can I write it up?"

But what I heard was:

"Lemme give you my card. Let me know what you want to do."

"The prices are marked on each bike. Call me over if you've got a question."

"If you decide, let me know."

"Thanks for coming in."

We didn't buy a bike for a month. My daughter was driving me nuts. I was afraid she was going to start calling bike stores in advance, saying: "If my dad and I come in, make sure somebody asks us to buy."

Nice people worked in most of the bike stores we visited. A lot of them knew bicycles inside-out. But their sales skills were just a little lacking.

The same thing applies to the mobile DJ industry. You can know everything there is to know about every aspect of the DJ business. But if you don't ask customers for the sale, if you don't ask them to book you, you're losing a lot of business.

You don't need to know 67 closes. You don't need a degree in salesmanship. You don't have to be a silver-tongued superstar. You just have to have the assertiveness, the guts and the smarts to ask customers to buy.

Maybe you should have a big sign above your phone that reads: "Ask the caller to book now!"

In the Bible it says: "Ask and you shall receive." In sales, sometimes it's, "If you don't ask, you don't receive." Ask at the first sign of acceptance. If the customer says, "That sounds just like what we're looking for," you can say, "Great, shall I go ahead and put you down for that date?"

It can be that simple. Often, all you have to do is ask.

Recognizing That If You Can't Close, Nothing Else You Do Right Matters

The close is where all of your hard work comes together. This is what matters the most. The point of doing everything else is to make the sale. But prospects don't want to be sold, they want to buy.

The days of high-pressure selling and bulldozing prospects into buying are over. To prospects, high pressure is "used-car" selling and to most it's a turn off. They may like what you have to offer immensely, but your tactics could ruin the sale. If you think it's pressure, it is. Don't try to remember "sure-sell" closes. Your prospect has probably heard them before and they won't get you the sale.

Instead of applying pressure where you don't need it, try using some basic sales skills. Everyone is a potential prospect, but not everyone is a potential customer. Learn how to qualify your prospects. To do this, you need to learn a lot about the people you're speaking with.

Have they ever used a DJ before? What type of music do they like? What kind of event are they interested in? What are they really looking for?

Qualifying Tie-Downs

When you're with a prospect, try for several minor "yeses" before you go for the big question. That's what *tie-downs* do. A tie-down is a question of confirmation tacked on a sentence, as in:

Qualifying

Qualification is the art of determining your prospect's wants and needs so that you can successfully explain the services you have to offer.

Initial qualification areas include:

- What type of event are you planning?
- What is your budget?
- How many people are you expecting?
- What age range of guests will you have?

Asking relevant questions is one of the keys to effective selling. Prudent use of time is another. This is why you want to become skilled with using all the qualifying questions you can. Adapt the style and question to your personality and the personality of the prospect.

Basic *Creative* Sales Skills Are a Necessity

- "That's a great package, isn't it?"
- "Those dancers would liven up your party, wouldn't they?"

If what you say represents truth as your prospects see it, they should respond by agreeing. If they agree on the quality and they agree that the benefits you're showing them meet their needs, they've moved closer to buying, haven't they? Here are some standard tie-downs:

Aren't they?	Aren't you?	
Can't you?	Couldn't it?	
Doesn't it?	Don't you agree?	Don't we?
Didn't it?	Isn't it?	Shouldn't it?
Wasn't it?	Isn't that right?	Won't it?
Wouldn't it?	Hadn't we?	

There are others, of course. You can also invert tie-downs or put them in the middle of a statement. Here are a couple of examples with tie-downs in the middle:

- "When you take advantage of this package for your awards dinner, *can't you* just picture all of the fun you and your friends will have?"
- "Since you plan to have people of various ages at your daughter's bat mitzvah, *won't it* be great to have this large playlist of songs to choose from?"

You can do many things with tie-downs, but it's extremely important not to overuse them. They're effective until they grate on people. One more caution.

When you use a tie-down, always wait for a positive reaction. Otherwise, you could "tie them down" to a negative reaction. Once you recognize the opportunities, you can use any of these tie-downs to keep your interview moving to the big Y-E-S.

The Art of Conversation

Always listen to your prospects. Many sales have been lost through lack of communication. What are they really saying to you? Pay attention. Talk to them about themselves. People love to hear themselves talk. While they talk, you listen.

If you're at a loss for things to ask your customers, try asking questions that begin with: who, what, where, when, why, or how. These are questions that require more than a "yes" or "no" response and will get your prospect talking with you.

Find out everything you can about your prospects. The more you know, the better able you will be to qualify them. Also, the more you know about each prospect, the better you will be able to understand their perceptions. You will be in a better position to tell what their statements: "Give me your card. I want to think about it," or "I want to check with my boss," really mean. That is: if they are really interested or if they just want to get away from you.

When you feel that you have sufficient information to qualify the buyer from the non-buyer, try to get the booking. You'll never know if they're going to book you unless you ask.

Compliment Your Way to a Sale

I once heard that the easiest way to get people to like you is to find something that you truly like about them, then compliment them on it. Sometimes it can be tough. Do you remember your mother telling you, "If you can't say something nice about somebody, don't say anything at all"? You can't sell anything to anybody by keeping your mouth shut. Some mobile DJs never seem to get over this hurdle. Others seem to excel at it.

One of the problems is that we never know what might offend someone. I remember going into a K-Mart store to buy an electric can opener. After looking at all the models on display, I had a question. The only clerk I could find couldn't help me, so she called the office for assistance. The next thing I knew, there was a page yelling out, "Would someone help the gray-haired man in housewares?" I bolted for the door. Maybe I've got gray hair, but sometimes to me it's light brown. I don't remember getting gray. Gray is for old people. I'm not old. Don't remind me about it.

I went into a Sears store in a mall the other day with my mom. I wanted to buy her an answering machine. We saw what we wanted in a case in the electronics section. Price had no bearing. Ease of purchase was the main concern. I went over to a young lady whom I had obviously taken away from daydreaming about her next break. I told her I'd like to buy the answering machine in the case. She told me she didn't have the keys. The person with the keys was at lunch. She didn't know what to do. I'd have to come back. And then she looked at me like I should have known better than to ask about an item that was under lock and key. Too bad for me.

So we went to the other side of the mall to a small electronics store. As soon as we went inside, a gentleman came over, greeted us, and told my mom how nice she looked. My mom is well over 80, and she beamed from head to toe. Heck, forget buying one answering machine, we'll buy two. Never mind the basic unit, let's go for the better models. It's amazing what a sincere compliment can do.

Last week I went to buy a golf shirt at Nordstrom in Pasadena, California. Now, I can buy a golf shirt from Penney's for $29. The Pro Shop at our club usually has $39 golf shirts on sale for $55. (Support your local pro.) So I guess I was prepared to spend up to 60 bucks. I went to the menswear department, took a shirt off the rack, and tried it on. When I came out of the dressing room to look at it in the big mirror, the clerk said that the shirt fit, but what did I think about the style? I didn't know. My youngest daughter always tells me what's cool and what's not, and she wasn't with me. So I asked him, "What about the style?" He said it was a more mature look, and I seemed to be a younger guy. I liked this person already.

I asked him what he suggested, and he took me to a table with the new Calloway shirt line. He showed me a silk golf shirt. It had a lining and unique buttons. The pattern was outstanding. I went in to try it on, and when I came out, the clerk said: "Wow, that looks absolutely great on you. You could wear it to play golf or underneath a sport coat. You look like a golfer—being tall and thin. You probably have a lot of golf shirts, if you play all the time. Are you close to scratch? Is your handicap in single digits? You certainly look like you play the game." That's it. Sold.

I took out my credit card, had it rung up *and then looked at the price.* A hundred and ten dollars! I thought to myself, "Am I crazy? A hundred and ten bucks for a golf shirt?" Of course I didn't say it quite that way. Instead I said, "I could tell by the quality that it must be rather expensive." I signed the charge slip, smiled, and then very carefully carried it in the bag so the shirt wouldn't get wrinkled.

Now when I wear the shirt and somebody tells me how good it looks, I always say, "thanks ... guess how much it cost?" I love to say, "It was

$110." I feel bad when somebody guesses the price. And I wouldn't have bought it without the compliments from the clerk. You never know what a compliment will do for you.

Try this. The next time you're talking to a prospect, compliment him or her. "You seem to be very knowledgeable about music. Have you ever worked in the industry? Your personal music collection must be very large. What do you think of (name some new artist or one related to the type of music you've been discussing)? I can tell that having the right music for your event will be very important to you. Let me show you my song list..."

If someone comes in with a bad attitude and tries to make you their entertainment for the afternoon, it could be very tough to come up with a compliment. When all else fails, just smile. Before long they'll want to know what you're smiling about, and they'll start smiling too. And then you can tell them they must be a very astute shopper, or they know your industry inside out, or maybe you just wanted to tell them they look nice. Maybe it's their clothes, their hair, their personality, their watch or their car. OK. OK. Maybe they have bad breath, green teeth, bratty kids, and questionable credit. Well, you can't just ignore them. You want them to be your friends. Find something about them you really like. Everybody has some redeeming qualities. At least that's what I've heard. Compliment them. And you'll compliment your way right into a sale.

You Need Better-Than-Basic Sales Skills

Some mobile DJs don't like to think of themselves as "salespeople." They think it makes them look pushy or less than professional.

Well, you don't have to be pushy to sell. But you do have to be professional. And that means helping your customers choose the right services for their event and then asking them to buy.

One of the biggest problems mobile DJs have is asking for the booking. This doesn't have to be difficult. All you need to do is recommend the appropriate package, and then ask: "Would you like it?" Then wait for their answer. Too many DJs get nervous at this stage and talk themselves right out of the booking.

Ask them to buy, and then practice listening. You have to wait for an answer. Just don't jump in with more dialogue. Too much talking can kill a sale.

Cleaning Up the Sale

Cleaning up the sale refers to the professional practice of being sure that there's no misunderstanding or confusion in the customer's mind. After all the papers are signed and before customers leave your meeting, review all the promises you've made.

Potential problems that may require clarification include:

- Promised length of gig: Do your customers understand when you're going to start playing and when you're going to stop? Do they know what the charge will be if they decide to add another hour at the event?
- Unintentional exaggerated claims: In your enthusiasm to make the sale, did you say something you weren't sure of? If so, now is the time to set the record straight.
- Special claims: If you made a promise, put it in writing and make sure it gets done.

Sometimes when writing up the contract, the DJ or the customer may have become nervous. After it's signed, both parties relax; and communication becomes easier. Use this relaxed time to solve any misunderstandings that may cause problems later.

Rejection

Sometimes, even if you've done everything right, a prospect won't book you. When your prospect says no, don't let the rejection get you down. You can't sell to everyone.

Basic *Creative* Sales Skills Are a Necessity

Ask yourself often, "What business am I in?" You are not just in the DJ business. You are in a business that enhances the lives of others. It's show business. You help people make important events successful. What you do is important. Create new ideas to sell to your customers. Keep the business exciting. You never know if an idea will work unless you try it.

Even though you want to be a friend to your prospects, you're still a competitor in the business. Keep thinking of better ways to do things. Stay ahead of the competition.

Keep a positive attitude. Henry Ford said: "Whether you think you can or think you can't, you're absolutely right." Believe that you can increase your bookings, and you will.

Questions & Thought-Starters

1) Think about how many closing techniques you know. How many do you really use? How many do you need to know?
2) How do *you* define qualifying?
3) List 10 qualifying questions you can ask prospects.
4) What are some of the things you should look at when qualifying prospects?
5) List some ways to get your prospects talking with you.

Being defeated is often a temporary position. Giving up is what makes it permanent.

—Marilyn vos Savant

Overcoming Objections

What causes objections? One theory of salesmanship says that if a sale is well organized—if the preliminary work and the presentation are right—there should be no objections. To some extent, that may be true, but as long as people differ from one another, we will always have natural "objectors." There are, for instance, prospects who even object to you calling them to follow up a lead. No sooner do you call them than they tell you why they can't hear what you have to say. They are too busy; they are on their way out of town; they know all about your service, etc. Those are not objections. They are, as you know, only excuses. They are to be expected.

If you do meet objections, politely ask your prospects, "Why?" or "Why's that?" Get them to explain why they are not interested in booking you. Objections can be very valuable. They let you know what the customer is thinking.

When you find that your presentation is meeting too many objections, do some heavy thinking. Constantly recurring objections don't just happen; maybe your sales presentation is at fault. A leading psychologist analyzed over 1,000 objections encountered by a group of salespeople. He found that more than half of them were the result of the salesperson's own mental attitude and had nothing to do with the prospect's intent to buy. In other words, the objection was put in the prospect's mouth by some negative thought in the salesperson's mind.

What are these negative things? There are many of them. Perhaps you are overconfident and show it. Maybe family problems or a flat tire have jangled your nerves; or heavy traffic on the way to the appointment has made you particularly irritable. In these instances, you should put these thoughts behind you, realizing that they have nothing to do with the business at hand.

The very fact that we allow ourselves to hold negative thoughts about prospects is an invitation for objections. Strive for an attitude toward people that will make them like you and believe what you say. That's one of the secrets of overcoming objections in selling. The right kind of attitude toward the buyer will dispose of the objection before it is ever made.

Objections You'll Probably Hear

Objections are valuable. Without them, you have either an easy sale or no sale. Objections are statements or questions that prospects give as reasons why they:

Would book now ... if the price were better, or if they were convinced they really wanted you.

Won't book now ... because they might decide later, or because they don't have time.

Shouldn't book now ... because your service costs too much.

Will book later ... after checking budget, or after going to the committee or other decision-maker.

Could book ... they like you and can afford your services, but want to think it over.

Can't book ... because they have no money, and have no credit.

Objection Categories

- **Stalls** are objections that prospects give just to get away from you or because they can't make a decision.

- **Genuine** objections are legitimate reasons for not buying. Prospects have no money, no credit, or they simply don't like your service.

Overcoming Objections

- **Genuine indecision** objections are not stalls; the customers just aren't convinced. They're still committed to finding more information.
- **Lack of desire** objections can be the result of a poor presentation, or perhaps the prospects are not convinced that they want a DJ.
- **Phony** objections are those that hide a real reason.

Good salespeople use objections to find out what they need to do to sell. Weak salespeople use objections as alibis to justify why prospects didn't buy. You can either believe all objections, or you can learn to intelligently benefit from them and use them to your advantage in closing sales. Each objection provides an opportunity to target your approach to the prospect's concerns and doubts. Before attempting to overcome an objection, you need to consider some of these possibilities:

- Is it a real objection?
- Is it the only objection?
- Do I need to get a commitment from the customer before solving the problem?
- Does the objection point out a customer's inability to make a decision?
- If they hang up or leave now, will I ever talk to them again?

Some DJs fear objections, especially if they lack the ability to accurately categorize the type of objection they are dealing with. Here is a partial list of objections you can consistently expect to encounter:

"We have several other aspects of the event to arrange. We'll call you back in about three months."

"I'll have to ask my husband."

"We'll have to check our budget."

"We never make snap decisions."

"You're the first DJ we've talked to."

"It's too much money."

"I can't give you a deposit until my income tax refund arrives."

"We're going to go with a DJ, and when we're ready, we'll definitely call you."

"Your competitor made a better offer."

"We'll think it over. Give us your card and we'll call you."

You would probably have a mental collapse if you tried to develop a solution for each of these objections. Fortunately, you don't have to. A common denominator exists among them. In every case, the prospect is implying something. Without further clarification you would have to assume or interpret their intent.

None of the objections on this list is explicit. There are only two statements prospects might make that would be explicit in a closing situation. If they said, "Yes, I'll book you," or "No, I don't want to book you," and turned and walked away ... that would be explicit. In either of these cases, there is no further need for verification. But in all of the objections on the above list, there remains some vagueness.

For example, if prospects say, "We'll have to check our budget," you need to pin down whether or not they really want to use you, what price range they think is appropriate, how long it will take to check their budget, and what you can do to help.

Most objections are not invitations for an argument, but rather requests for more information. By supplying the proper information, you may very likely earn a sale. When you train yourself to view objections in this way, they will not intimidate you. Instead they will steer you in the proper direction to finalize the sale.

Confronting Price-Value Objections

Most DJs are going to promise the same things to customers. They'll promise music, a sound system, a professional look, and so on. So if you want to differentiate yourself from your competition, and get your price, you have to go deeper into the prospect's concerns. Tell the customer that you're going to take away all of his or her pressure and stress. Make things easier for your customers. That's what they're looking for. Price is secondary.

When someone says, "Your price is too high," you're probably dealing with a perception problem. If you fail to convert the features that you offer into customer benefits, you may hear some objections such as these:

- "I don't pay full price for anything."
- "I'm sure you can do better than that."
- "We could get a band for that much."
- "It's too much money."
- "Another DJ gave me a better deal."

In each of these cases, the prospect has not estimated the value of your services to equal what you are charging. If you had completely sold them on your services, their judgment of value should equal or exceed your price tag. By asking you for a discount, they are urging you to compromise your price to meet whatever shortage in benefits your presentation created. The top DJs normally sell at the top price because they have a strong ability to communicate benefits and, therefore, are not forced to adjust their price.

You may need to be more detailed in your description of your services. Explain things like, "We arrive and set up before any of your guests get there," or "We'll give you a tape of your daughter

Overcoming Objections

when she's blowing out the candles at her sweet sixteen party." These may be things you do automatically, but if you don't tell your customers that you do them, they'll have no way of knowing.

You also have to differentiate yourself from your competitors. (Remember, you're all promising the same basics.) Think about what sets you apart. Maybe another DJ advertises that he has 1,000 CDs to choose from. In that case, tell your customers that you guarantee that you will have all of their requests.

When I started selling many years ago, I was always terrified at quoting a price that I believed myself was too high. Particularly when I was selling a new model or product that I wasn't that familiar with. To make it easy for myself, and to help overcome that fear of waiting for a response after mentioning the price, I came up with sort of a cushion for my apprehensiveness. What I did was quote the price, wait a couple of seconds until it sank into the customer's brain, and then said, "You're probably wondering why it's so cheap, aren't you?" Once in awhile I would hear, "Heck no, that's a lot of money." But more often than not, I would hear, "We really were not sure what something like that would cost," or "Well, it seems like we get a lot for the price." Both responses would immediately lead into a discussion of value versus price. Once the shock of the price was past, it was easy to get into features and benefits and asking for the sale.

When a customer starts saying things like: "That's a lot of money," or "Your price is too high," your mental thought pattern should go to: "Compared to what?" Let me give you a case in point. Last Saturday I stopped in at Sakes Fifth Avenue to buy a couple of shirts. Saks is at 50th and Fifth in New York City, the heart of the big-time merchandising stores. I went to the second floor to buy a couple of black dress T-shirts. You know, the kind worn underneath a blazer to look like you're trendy, even if you're not. At JCPenney they are around $12. The Gap has them for about $15. Geoffrey Beane will cost you about $20. On the rack at Saks were satin-finished T-shirts at $98. I looked twice. $98!! A clerk who could be a young Mike Tyson (only with better teeth and diction) came over, and I said, "Do you have anything else like this?"

He said, "Well, if you want something with style, you might try the sixth floor. That's our European collection. The elevators are to the left."

So I went up to the sixth floor. I knew it was the "trendy, what's happening, so-cool-you-can't-stand-it" floor, because the nonstop alternative rock music along with the glare of the pin spots and floodlights on every piece of clothing could give you headache. There were styles and fashions by Ermenegildo Zegna, Gianni Versace, Brioni, Loro Piana and Salvatore Ferragamo.

The prices were the cutting edge of fashion as well. I went over to the Versace display and found a black T-shirt. I picked it up and saw the price tag. $545! (You read it right, $545!!) I couldn't believe it. A clerk came over (this one looked like Niles from the television show "Frasier") and asked if he could be of assistance.

I was still trying to overcome severe price-tag shock. All that I could think of to say was, "I thought this might be long-sleeved." And with a flash, he produced the same shirt with long sleeves from behind the counter. Of course, it was a little more pricey—$610. It sure made the $98 one on the second floor seem like a real bargain.

So I went back down to see the Mike Tyson look-alike. It was as if he was waiting for me. I told him about the T-shirts I had seen, and he took me over to another section to show me a Saks line of shirts for $45. I bought three. It seemed like a steal. He then asked if I had a Saks charge. I didn't. He told me that if I opened one right then, everything I purchased that day would be an additional 10 percent off. I did. And then he suggested a couple of sweaters, a tomato-colored sweater vest ... my purchases were piling up. And just when I thought there was nothing else he could suggest, he asked, "Hey, where's your umbrella? It's going to be raining. Didn't you see the weather forecast?"

I said I didn't have one. He said, "Come with me." We went down to the first floor. Umbrellas. $20.

He said, "Here, add this on. You need it. With your discount you'll save two bucks."

I'd hate to tell you what the bill totaled. And if I had gone in and saw a $45 black T-shirt originally, without any assistance, I probably never would have bought anything. Top-down selling. Expensive compared to what?

Don't be afraid to tell customers the price for your top-of-the-line package. Help them put your price into perspective by comparing it to the cost of a live band. Tell them what they get: fog machines, light towers, confetti guns, karaoke, limitless music selection, nonstop music with no breaks, etc., compared to a band. Before long, they'll believe you're offering them a great deal.

When They've Already Been Shopping

If prospects immediately tell you that they've already been talking to other mobile DJs, you might want to ask them these three questions: Who have you seen? Who have you seen that you've really liked? and Why didn't you book them? This will allow you to see their true objections.

I thought about the black Versace T-shirt at Saks for a long time. I went back the next day with my camera. Took a picture of me and the $545 undershirt. I asked the clerk how he could rationalize the price. What makes it that expensive? He told me it was 22-gauge breathable fabric. It was 4 percent spandex. And since Gianni Versace was recently murdered, it would hold its value and could conceivably be worth more later. I asked the clerk if he didn't think $545 for a T-shirt was a little outrageous. He confided in me that it was a little much. He said $375 would have been more in line. I think I'll go back to Penney's. Or at least to the second floor of Saks.

20 Things to Do Before Cutting the Price

Price is the most common objection mobile DJs hear. Too often, DJs try to overcome price objections by simply lowering the price—and their profit margins along with it. Here are 20 things to do before cutting your price.

1) Don't panic. Hold the conviction that your price is right. Fear of price is the weakest point in selling. If you aren't sure your price is fair, how can you convince your customers that it is? Confidence will win their respect.

2) Get all the facts. Check the local competition. What do they charge?

3) Find out if a customer is bluffing. Does he *really* have a better offer elsewhere?

4) Sell your service. Convince your customer that differences in quality justify your price.

5) Be flexible. Adjust the extras quoted, then refigure your price on the reduced package.

6) Look for a "catch" in a competitive price. It's nearly always there.

7) Show a different package. Then you and your competitor aren't figuring the same service.

8) Do things you do that no local competitor offers.

9) Discuss the equipment that you use. Someone can always offer an inferior product at a lower price.

10) Cite some examples of unhappy people who booked on price alone—there are plenty.

11) Sell your business. Emphasize all your good points—service, music selection, reputation. Salesmanship *can* win over price alone.

12) Be reasonable. Demonstrate the difference between price and value. Avoid arguments. Talk customer benefits.

13) Be sure to figure your own costs carefully to make sure you are on firm ground when price discussion becomes necessary.

Overcoming Objections

14) Offset a concession. Work for your customers. Make them feel that you are always trying to find ways to give them better service at a fair price.

15) If your history is better than your competitor's, ask the prospective buyer to check on your reputation for service, timeliness and general character.

16) Stand behind the service you give as part of your policy. If something goes wrong at a gig, tell customers that you will take responsibility personally.

17) Offer more. Offering extras sometimes gives you an opportunity to better the deal for the prospective buyer on an item you have to offer that your competitor doesn't.

18) Sometimes, a frank discussion of good business sense will show the prospects that your price is fair and that they'll get better service from a firm that operates on a sound financial basis with fair prices.

19) Think of the future. Consider the ethics and future results of cutting a price today. Are you willing to offer that price to other prospects? Consider the problems of cutting prices too often.

20) Always remember that in any price concession, every penny comes right out of your profits.

Legitimate Objections

Once you have developed the ability to understand what objections are and how they evolve in the selling situation, overcoming them is reasonably routine in most cases. You can't overcome all objections, but there is only one that keep prospects from buying if they really want to. It is:

No money.

If your prospects understand all of the benefits of your service and can afford it, logically, they should book. With no money, though, it's hard to put a deal together.

Handling Indecision

If you review the list of probable objections, you should now recognize that most of them either request more information, demonstrate that you have more work to do, or reveal your prospect's indecisiveness. In the first of these instances, simply give them the information and ask them to buy again. If you haven't developed value, go back to the basics.

One area that probably gives us more trouble than any other is prospects' reluctance to make a decision. Some prospects simply do not want to make a decision of consequence. It is far easier

Overcoming Objections

for them to walk away than it is to make a decision to purchase. In this case, we hear objections that sound like:

- "We'll have to check our budget."
- "We never make snap decisions."
- "This is our first time looking for a DJ."
- "We'll decide next month."
- "We'll think it over."
- "I want to go home and think about it."
- "My brother-in-law knows about music. I'll see what he says."
- "You're the first DJ I've talked to."

Basically, these prospects are saying, "I want to get away from you before I sign something or make a commitment." Keep your head together. Don't let customers blow a lot of smoke and convince you that you're inept at your job.

Knowing that the prospect is wrestling with the burden of making a decision, try to direct your approach out of the present situation into the future. In the present, prospects have to look at the decision presently confronting them. By looking into the future, they can make the *easier* decision of wanting to enjoy their event.

The word "suppose" is a very valuable tool to force the situation out of the present into the future. To suppose means to imagine, to consider as a possibility, to expect. You are attempting to hypothetically solve prospects' current problems, project them into ownership at a future date, and have them look back at the decision to book, acknowledging that they did the right thing by booking you. In other words, you want to paint a very strong positive mental picture of a time when the prospect is enjoying his or her event, and all of the benefits you've discussed have become a reality. Make prospects agree that if this were the case, they would have made a wise decision. Once they agree, ask them again to go ahead now, so the enjoyment can begin. If they say that they probably will book you, ask them to do it now: "Why don't we put it on paper and take a look at it?"

Overcoming objections doesn't have to be difficult. Treat them as windows into your prospects' minds and use them to determine what your prospect is thinking. When you know the reasons behind the objections, you can overcome them and make the sale.

Overcoming Objections

Questions & Thought-Starters

1) In what way are objections valuable?
2) List three general rules for handling objections.
3) What should you consider before attempting to overcome an objection?
4) What do you need to do when you encounter a price-value objection?
5) List the only objection that can keep prospects from buying.
6) How can you handle indecisive prospects?

10

You can get whatever you want if you help enough people get what they want.

—Zig Ziglar

Referral Selling and "Who Do You Know?"

In the DJ business, more prospects equal more sales. The more appointments you make and the more people you talk to, the more business you will do. There are a lot of ways to get more customers to meet with you. You can run ads, send out direct mail or spend big dollars on radio or television advertising. You can run major promotions, or you could take a lesson from life insurance salespeople. A local agency doesn't usually spend big bucks on drive-time radio, and I have yet to see an ad in a local paper that reads: "Special This Weekend: Whole Life 50 Percent Off!" When you sign up for a policy, they usually ask you to supply them with a name or two of people they can try to sell insurance to as well.

They might use different words, but the approach is basically the same. You're signing on the dotted line and they slip a little card in front of you explaining that "This is how I earn my living …

Referral Selling and "Who Do You Know?"

and since you've made a very wise decision, who else do you know (friends, work associates, family members) who could use this type of coverage? Please write their names down here."

When was the last time you asked a customer: "Who else do you know?" Do you ever ask? The easiest place to find more customers is to ask your existing customers for referrals. You can call it "referral selling," but it's really just common sense. Some mobile DJs do it. Most don't. How much business could you do, if you asked everyone you did a gig for: "Who else do you know?" You'd increase your business by at least 30 percent.

Let's say a DJ is writing up a major contract. What does he or she think about while writing it up? Probably something like:

1) How much money am I making on this deal?
2) I hope their check clears.
3) I hope they don't change their minds tomorrow.

Instead of wasting brain cells on these thoughts, the DJ could be asking the excited new clients who else they know who might be interested in booking a DJ for an upcoming event.

There's a magic time when you should ask for a referral. It's not when the event has been over for a month. It's not two days, two weeks or two months after the clients sign the contract. It's when the client's event has just ended and everyone had a wonderful time. Their enthusiasm will never be that high again.

It's like the people who buy a new car and finally take delivery. They check out everything on the car, play with the buttons, check out the features, set the clock and the radio, and then drive out of the lot. For the first time, they go the speed limit all the way home. They show it to their neighbors and everybody gets to go for a ride. They wash it the next day. But after a couple of weeks, it's no longer the same. They let the kids eat in the back seat. Their coffee spills on the carpet during the trip to work. The new-car smell is gone and the car takes on the odor of stale food. They're not that eager to take people for a ride around the block. The thrill starts to subside. It's just not the same anymore.

When clients hand you your check at the end of a successful event, you might say; "We get a lot of new customers from people like you who are happy with how well their events went. Who do you know (maybe neighbors, friends or relatives) who also might be interested in hiring a DJ?"

If you just stop for a minute and let the customers think, they'll probably come up with a name or two. It's really pretty easy, and since you've become their friend (you have, haven't you?) you'll find that most of the time, customers will be eager to help you out, since this is the way you earn your living. If they don't think of anyone on the spot, send them a comment card a week after the event asking their opinion of how the event went. Include a section for referrals. You can also call to follow up a week or so later.

It's easy after that. There are several things you can do, and several approaches you can take. You can call those people and tell them that your customer/friend suggested that you contact them. You can explain that their friends thought they might be in the market for a DJ as well. You want to help them. You're just doing your job. Suggest sending over a brochure. You want to be their friend as well.

Or you might want to just send a note first, introducing yourself and your company. Mention your satisfied customer's name and tell them you'll be calling to see if you can send information on your service. After you send the print material, follow it up with another phone call and ask for a possible appointment to give them some ideas on how you could help make their next event one to remember, and to answer any questions they might have.

If you can't get an appointment right away, don't give up. Call back again with additional information a few weeks later, or call back in a month or so with a new idea you might not have mentioned the first time. Sometimes you have to contact a referral several times before you can get any type of positive action.

OK, OK, everyone you call is not going to jump at the chance to meet you. But what if just a few did? How much would that add to your numbers at the end of the month?

This is not rocket science. They do it in the car business, the insurance business, and the mutual fund business. But I bet your competition doesn't do it. So the next time you finish a great gig, ask: "Who do you know...?" You'll add to your mailing list, increase your prospect list, and maybe get new customers through your doors. You may never have to advertise again.

Turning Clients into Torchbearers

Wouldn't it be great if every client you ever had told 10 more people to hire you as well? What if every person who left one of your gigs raved so much about your selection, personality, and talent that they turned into evangelists for your business? Think it's impossible? While you're thinking about whether it's impossible or not, consider the people who wear the Nike "swoosh" symbol on their hats and shirts, the Amway, Shaklee, Herbalife, or LCI multilevel marketing participants who preach the benefits and rewards of coming on board, and the

Referral Selling and "Who Do You Know?"

Harley-Davidson fanatics who tattoo the name of their favorite bike on their arms, chest and other extremities.

These people aren't just customers who have an interest in a product or store. These people have a belief, and one person with a belief is equal to a force of 99 who have an interest. Have you ever run into a devoted Macintosh user and asked why they prefer a Mac over an IBM PC? They can be one-person PR programs. These people have a passion for the product.

To turn your clients into torchbearers for your DJ service, you first must have something for them to rave about. Creating a "great, best-there-is" selection of music or "out-of-the-ordinary" service is the first step toward turning clients into evangelists for you and your business. And you'll never get clients to tell how much they love your service unless you have a passion for the job yourself. If you love what you're doing and understand your clients' needs, that's the start of a cause where your clients can help wave your flag for you.

Take this little quiz:

Do you feel that you offer the finest, "absolutely-without-a-doubt" best mobile DJ service in your market today?

Do you feel that no one can touch your business for value, service, and music selection?

Do you pursue your existing clients to bring them to a higher level of commitment?

Do you handle every client complaint, question, or dissatisfaction like the business of another 100 people will depend on it?

If a person who just booked you for a wedding next year tells you that she can get a cheaper DJ for the same date, do you rationalize your value versus price and make her a believer?

If you answered "no" to any of the questions, it's going to be difficult to create torchbearers and evangelists for your mobile DJ business. If the answers are all "yes," you're really on your way. If the answer is a huge, emphatic "YES!" you're probably there now and your clients are already spreading the word.

Have you ever seen the commercials for Troy-Bilt rototillers and grass cutters on TV? Troy-Bilt recruits owners of their machines to help sell their products. The owners don't actually "sell" the products, but they endorse them if a potential customer calls. And Troy-Bilt suggests that prospects call these people to see if they're happy. To answer questions. To give advice. These volunteer salespeople are part of the company's "Good Neighbor" program. Troy-Bilt recruits them at the time of pur-

Referral Selling and "Who Do You Know?"

chase by offering them a discount or free attachment. Troy-Bilt owners are evangelists about their machines and like to spread the good news. These torchbearers support the company by providing credible information to potential customers.

Applebee's restaurants train their servers to continually ask customers if everything is OK; if there is anything else they can do; if there is anything else they need. Not just once, but several times during the course of the meal. If there is a problem, the manager comes out, apologizes, and gets involved. If everything is not quite right, they make it right, and there is no check. The meal is free. The manager asks the customer to come back again and give them another chance. They turn an unhappy dinner guest into a torchbearer by having them tell all their friends … not that the meal was bad, but how the employees went out of their way to rectify it, to make them happy.

A local car wash has a neat way of creating torchbearers. They know the names of all their best customers and keep them on a computer data base according to license number. As the car is pulling up, they run the license plate number on their computer to find out the name of the customer and how many times the car has been in during the past few months. They make sure that the customers are called by name when they come in. Then they will comp a car wash every once in awhile. You never know. Once in awhile they will say, "It's

113

OK ... it's on us ... come back again." When the customer thanks them for the freebie, they say, "No problem, just send another customer our way. We want more people like you." It's a personal touch that no one else offers. They almost have a cult following.

You don't have to comp a gift to get referrals, but getting to know your clients better might be a start. With everybody carrying the torch for your DJ business, you won't have to spend hundreds of dollars on advertising just to get your phone ringing. Your clients and all the people they know can help do it for you.

Networking: The Power of Personal Contact

Networking is nothing more than staying in contact with people you know, particularly centers of influence (party planners, wedding coordinators, caterers, etc.) and talking to anyone who could be a potential client.

Your circle of influence is made up of your immediate family, your relatives, friends, neighbors, and the people you come into contact with every day. Try to think of people who would be in a position to know prospective clients. What circles of influence do your current clients have? Who are their friends? You'll be surprised at how many new clients you can meet by networking on a regular basis.

Referral Selling and "Who Do You Know?"

It's a matter of not only *who you know,* but *who knows you.* Think about it. Who can you know? When someone is ready to book a DJ, do they know who you are and how to reach you? Let people know who you are and what you do, so when they're in the market for a DJ—or if they know somebody who's in the market for a DJ—your name will be the first one they think of.

Join a local service club like Rotary, Kiwanis, or Lions. Offer to give free talks to any service or community group that will have you. Give a short talk to increase your personal visibility and business image. Talk about what you know best. Some topics might include:

- Entertaining Made Easy
- Building Your Music Library
- How to Do (the Latest Dance Craze)
- Make Your Next Anniversary Party (Wedding, Bar Mitzvah, etc.) More Fun

Be creative; choose a subject that people are interested in, and one that you can speak authoritatively on. Not only will you get a chance to build rapport and trust with the group, but you can walk away with the names and addresses of almost every member. All you have to do is put together a handout that members would be interested in receiving: a copy of an article, an interesting poster, or an audio cassette. At the conclusion of your talk, mention that this is available for those people who are interested. You can make it special by saying, "We can't afford to give these out to everyone we run into, but for those of you who are interested, we'd be happy to drop one of these in the mail to you at no charge, if you just leave your name and address on the table in back."

All these names cost you is the price of the item and the hour you took to give the speech. Keep these prospects in your database and include them in a "For our special friends..." mailing.

It's also helpful to join organizations like the National Association of Catering Executives (NACE). Most cities have a local chapter. Another organization to consider is the International Special Events Society (ISES). Whichever organization you join, attend the meetings and network with the other members. It's easier to call a planner you've already met and say, "Hi, this is Bill Jones, we met at the NACE function last week. I was wondering if we could line up an appointment where I could tell you more about my DJ service," than it would be to call the same person cold. It's also a good idea to join your local chamber of commerce for the same reasons.

And remember, the more people who know what you do for a living, the more customers you'll have coming through your doors.

Who Do You Know?

Where do you look to find more prospects and clients when there's no one left to talk to? Everyone has their own circle of influence. These are the people you go to, not just for business, but for referrals as well. Keep in touch with these people on a regular basis to increase your business.

- Who do you know ... from your old job? ...from school or college? ... through your kids? ... because you rent or own your home?
- Who do you go dancing with?
- Who do you hunt or fish with?
- Who has sold you ... suits? ... a car? ... your glasses?
- Who did you receive a letter from today?
- Who did you write checks to this year?
- Who owns ... a music store? ... a grocery store? ... a shoe store? ... a wedding gown store? ... a dry cleaners? ... a party center? ... a retirement center? ... a business that's booming?
- Who is ... your barber/hairdresser? ... your jeweler? ... your dentist? ... your florist? ... a new neighbor? ... in your club ... on your Christmas list? ... a caterer? ... a meeting planner? ... your physician? ... a party planner? ... a high school principal? ... a teacher?
- Who manages or runs ... a movie theater? ... your bank? ... the local fitness club?
- Who was at your wedding?
- Who took your latest family photos?
- Who is having a class reunion?

Questions & Thought-Starters

1) What can you learn from insurance salespeople? Who else can you learn from? How could you use some of their techniques to book more gigs?

2) When's the best time to ask customers for referrals?

3) What can you do to turn your customers into advocates for your DJ service?

4) List three ways to contact referrals.

5) Go through the "Who Do You Know" list and answer the questions. Then add your own categories and fill them in. Now start contacting the people you've listed.

6) How would you define "networking"?

7) List five topics you can speak about for local community groups. Then work up a letter you can send to these groups offering to give your presentation at an upcoming meeting.

11

The bitterness of poor quality and service remains long after the sweetness of low price is forgotten.

—John Ruskin

Customer Service as a Sales Tool

If you want to increase your mobile DJ business dramatically within a very short period of time, you might want to start by bringing your customer service up a notch. The only problem is: different customers have different ideas of customer service. What might be important to one may have no bearing on another. Some people will never stop at a restaurant that has a letter out in its neon sign. Some customers will be reluctant to buy from a salesperson who has a lit cigarette on his desk. For many customers, personal attention is what matters. Let me give you an example.

I've been shopping at the same supermarket for the past few years. Lately, the checkout clerks seem to be getting less and less friendly. They scan the groceries, talk to their friends, and never look you in the eye. Last week, my bill came to $106.97. The clerk never looked up. She wouldn't smile. When she gave me my change, I started to leave with my groceries, but then I turned back and said: "You didn't say 'thank you.'" She said, "It's printed on the receipt."

Well, having it printed on the receipt is a far cry from saying it. I don't care if they have a bigger store, I'm not going back.

Attitude Really Makes the Difference

Attitude is a big part of customer service. A new McDonald's just opened up not too far from where I live. It's not the ordinary, everyday McDonald's, but more of a theme park, virtual-reality, "Ronald McDonald-on-steroids" wondercenter. They've been advertising on radio, TV and in all the local print media. They're giving away all kinds of prizes like trips to Paris, movie passes, home entertainment equipment, and a Rolls Royce. Well, not really a Rolls. I just made that up. But with all the hype, it sure seemed like everything was on "larger-than-life" scale.

I stopped there for lunch the other day. There were a ton of people. There were so many people that I had a hard time finding where the lines to the cash registers really were. Finally, I got to the counter where a young lady who looked like she may have just signed up for her driver's permit asked if she could help me.

Customer Service as a Sales Tool

As I ordered, she kept being distracted by another young person screaming orders and instructions from the kitchen area. At the same time, another teenager with a Madonna-type headset came running by screaming, "Where the hell are the fries? I need fries!"

Someone else turned and yelled, "Get your own damn fries; I just had to box my own apple pies."

It wasn't pleasant. I ordered a salad and my server said, "We don't have any made-up salads left. It will take a while. Want anything else?"

I didn't want to ruin her whole day, so I ordered something else, along with an apple pie.

She said, "They're two for a dollar."

I said, "I only want one."

She groaned and said, "OK, I'll try to work it out."

I could see that dividing by two was a real problem for her.

In the midst of more screaming and yelling from the back, and a little hissing, snarling and screeching at the front counter, my order came up. But it had two apple pies.

Foolishly I called it to the attention of Miss Out-of-Control, who said, "Well, what do you want me to do about it? They're two for a dollar."

Not wanting to make her day any worse than it obviously was already, I picked up one of the boxes and said, "Let's see; it says on your name tag that your name is Jessica?"

She replied, "Yeah ... ?"

So I took out a pen and wrote on the box: "To Jessica, from Bob." And since it was the holiday season, I wrote: "Happy Holidays!" And since I was on a roll, I drew a smiley face.

She looked at me and said, "Think you're cute, don't you?"

Well, the answer is "yes." I think I can be cute, funny, easygoing, semi-charming and a little on the less-than-serious side. When I'm the customer, I guess I can be whatever I want to be at the time.

McDonald's had gotten me into their megaburger playscape palace the first time, but I'm not going back. At least not for a long time. At least not until Jessica finds a job that is less demanding and maybe one where "works well with others" is not part of the criteria for advancement.

Now don't get me wrong. The food was OK. It was typical McDonald's fare. The price was ... heck, I don't even know what the price was. I don't know how much McDonald's charges for a Coke, or a shake, or fries, or a Big Mac. I don't care. I order, give them money, and sometimes I get change. Price is not an issue. I had to get two of something, even though I wanted one of something. Big deal. It's not the end of the world. But attitude is what brings people back.

You can have the lowest prices, the biggest musical selection, and the most exotic light show. You can have slick direct-mail, an easy-to-remember phone number, and state-of-the-art equipment. You'll get people calling, and may even book them the first time. But customers would rather go to the dentist for a root canal than to go back to a DJ with a rotten attitude.

Customers go back to (and refer their friends to) DJs they like, who treat them well, and who have smiles on their faces, and a good attitude about their jobs. Customers don't like to face DJs who wish they worked someplace else, are having a bad day, or can't wait until it's time to go home.

In this business, people call you to handle something that means a lot to them. Money can be an issue, but more often than not, it is not the main issue. People use a DJ they can trust. They hire DJs who know their music and equipment inside out and who really love the business they're in. They go out of their way to avoid DJs who complain about their job or have the weight of the world on their shoulders. And they hate to deal with DJs who are continually having a bad day.

Do a quick attitude check. What's your "smile" frequency? Do you really like your job? Would you rather be in another line of work? When you wake up in the morning, are you really anxious to get to a gig, or would you rather be doing something else? When customers tell you they can get a DJ for their event for $100 less, how do you react? Do you start to simmer inside? And when you lose a job to a competitor, do you take it out on your next customer? Do you carry any personal problems from home to work?

When business slows down or when your competition is breathing down your neck, how do you react? Do you lash back, sneer and snarl and wish you were doing something else? Or do you hang in there with a good attitude, knowing things will get better?

Abraham Lincoln once said, "It's not what happens to you, it's how you handle what happens to you that determines your happiness in life." Life's too short to have to deal with a bad attitude. Particularly when it's yours. A good attitude will help bring customers back. With a bad attitude, you may never see them (or their friends) again.

Customer Service Builds Loyalty

I had an interesting phone call a few days ago from a friend who's moving her office into an area

Customer Service as a Sales Tool

serviced by the telephone company GTE. Getting her service started in the new location has been somewhat of a mind-boggling experience. Remember Lily Tomlin's telephone operator "Ernestine" character on "Laugh-In"? Her classic phrase, "We don't have to be nice, we're the phone company," comes to mind.

When my friend called GTE, she was put through a "press-this-for-that" phone maze. After pushing enough buttons to make even an elevator operator crazy, a recording came on and said, "All lines are busy ... an attendant will be with you shortly." This was repeated every 20 seconds for a period of eight minutes. Eight minutes is not "shortly." Then all of a sudden, a voice came on and said, "I am experiencing heavy call volume at this moment, please give me your name and phone number, and I will call you back within 48 hours." She thought it was a computer and gave her name, only to hear, "How do you spell that?" It wasn't a computer at all: it was a person who spoke in a staccato monotone. This person took her name and phone number, and after two days, no one had called her back.

So much for customer service. GTE had trained this person, but even the most highly trained people only give lip service if there is no follow-through. Promise less. Deliver more. Follow through. If the attendant had said someone would get back to her in three days, and someone

125

had then called back in two, my friend would have been a happy customer. Saying two days and not calling back in four makes a customer want to slap somebody.

Remember "a baker's dozen"? Buy a dozen donuts and get 13. Makes for a happy customer. Opening the bag to find only 11 will make a customer angry. Finding 12 is OK ... that's what the customer expects. But a customer will tell his friends and probably go back again and again if there is one more for free. Over-deliver. Under-promise.

The best car dealers in the country have service departments that always do something for free, each time you come in. If you're only in for an oil change, maybe they check the belts for free. And it's shown as "no charge" on the bill. If it's a tune-up, maybe they'll wash the car and shampoo the mats at no charge. "Free" shows on the bill. Give customers more than they expect.

When people hire you, they expect reasonable prices, decent music selection, and pleasant service. Give them more than they're expecting. Show up early. Play for an extra 10 minutes. Find a copy of that special song they requested.

Remember this: Customer service is not customer service if there is no follow-through. You can promise the world, but the customer won't care if you only give lip service. Give more than

Customer Service as a Sales Tool

the customer expects. Customers like to hear phrases such as:

"We'll take care of it right away."

"We're glad to do it at no charge."

"Here's something we'd like to throw in for free."

"We want to make you happy."

And the list goes on. Giving customers more than they expect will not only get you repeat business, it will get you more business, because your customers will be so impressed, they'll tell their friends. Your local utility company never says "Here's an extra week of service on us. No charge." It doesn't happen. The phone company has become a mechanical computer monster. And most grocery stores don't carry groceries out to your car any more. That's why those carts roll into your car and ding your door. Go one better than everyone else. Find out what your competition is doing, then just do it a little bit better, a little bit faster. But don't set your customer up for a disappointment. Not only do what you say, do just a bit more. Promise realistically. Deliver more. And watch the customers line up at your door or ring your phone off the hook.

What do your clients *want?* What do they *expect?* To increase your mobile DJ business by 30 percent or more, it's up to you to find out. Customer service starts by exceeding your customers' expectations. What are your customers looking for? Check out your competition. What makes them stand out? How can you be better? In customer service, there is a "first-mover advantage." If you can be the first one to offer a better service in a certain area, you can stay ahead of the pack for a long time... but not forever. Periodic self-evaluation is necessary.

Today's customers are not very loyal. There's really no such thing as a "customer-for-life" anymore. The reality is that most customers go where they feel they are getting the most value. Today, your main goal is to capture your customer for a period of time with every conceivable strategy and technique. But there isn't one single strategy that will make you stand out as the best mobile DJ in your area. It's going to take a combination of things, and the DJ with the best combination of customer service strategies and techniques will be around *and profitable* for a long time.

We have a Saturn dealership in town. Now, Saturn has developed a reputation for good customer service. The company consistently scores at least 90 percent when customers are surveyed on how pleased they are with their new cars and with their car-buying experience.

Part of the company's customer-service success comes from its proactive approach. Saturn asks its customers what they want, then delivers. And sometimes they don't even wait for customer suggestions. Our local Saturn customer assistance liaison said in a recent newspaper article: "We sit around sometimes and think about what new thing we can offer, and create a service we hadn't been asked for." That's how the dealerships' courtesy car washes began.

It's a great example of figuring out what you can do to exceed customer expectations and then doing it. Sometimes a little brainstorming, taking a second look at what you're doing now, is all that's necessary.

Think about what you can do to better meet your customers' needs and to help your DJ business stand out from the others. How can you make things easier for your customers. One easy idea to implement would be coming up with an event planner that you could give your customers. It doesn't have to be anything fancy, maybe just a folder with some checklists and ideas. You could have one for weddings, another for bar/bat mitzvahs, another for anniversary parties—whatever you do the most of. Giving them a planner shows your customers that you want to help them make their events as good as they can be.

Check out the following list. How many of these things depict your DJ business the way it is today? How many of these things did you do at one time, but stopped? It's important to periodi-

129

cally stop and take a look at your business through the eyes of a customer.

Self-Analysis

Answer yes or no to the following questions. How do you stack up?

☐ Yes ☐ No **I am easy for clients to get ahold of. I have an answering machine and pager for times when no one is in the office.**

Today you have to be available for clients who juggle full-time jobs and less free time. You have to cater to the customers' hours ... even weeknights and Sundays if necessary. If you don't, someone else could acquire your prospects and customers.

☐ Yes ☐ No **My office is in an easy-to-find and convenient location.**

Are directions easy to give to your office? If not, you may be losing clients along the way to your location. If people can't figure out where your office is or how to get to it, they'll go somewhere they can find.

Customer Service as a Sales Tool

☐ Yes ☐ No   Our office is neat and clean, and we have someone who checks to make sure it is spotless every day.

A dirty office and dusty displays contradict the image you want to give to your customers, and take away from the value of your service.

☐ Yes ☐ No   We offer a meaningful guarantee that addresses consumers' true concerns and puts our reputation on the line, every time.

Standing behind your work to the nth degree will separate you from the competition and make customers want to refer others to you. Doing expert work will assure that you will rarely be taken up on your guarantees. But having guarantees shows that you are responsible.

☐ Yes ☐ No   Everyone on my staff is well-trained, and we continually provide training on an ongoing basis.

When you're green you're growing; when you're ripe you rot. You need ongoing learning on a regular basis to keep your staff up-to-date on the latest trends and techniques in the industry. Your employees aren't much help to customers if they are unaware of the latest dances, new music, or how to use your newest equipment. Your customers want to know that your employees are on the cutting edge: that they can rely on them for up-to-date advice.

☐ Yes ☐ No **DJs are not permitted to drink at a gig.**

Your DJ's behavior at a gig reflects on your entire company. Even if they "just have one," or are encouraged to drink by the hosts, drinking alcoholic beverages while working is not professional behavior.

☐ Yes ☐ No **Employees are not permitted to smoke in the office or at a gig.**

It's a sign of keeping up with the times and being aware of how to make a pleasant experience for your customers. Employees also should not be allowed to smoke near the office entrance or outside the door of a gig. It doesn't look professional.

Customer Service as a Sales Tool

☐ Yes ☐ No   I write my home phone number on the back of my business card when giving one to a prospect.

You want your customers to know that you are always available for them. Don't have your home phone number printed on the cards, or write it on ahead of time. The gesture has more power if you write it on the card in front of the prospect.

☐ Yes ☐ No   I make it easy for customers to buy.

Customers are more likely to buy when you make it easy for them to afford to do so. Some people are uncomfortable paying a large amount of cash upfront. Are checks OK? Do you accept credit cards?

☐ Yes ☐ No   All of my employees are appropriately dressed.

What would you think if your doctor came into the examining room wearing a T-shirt with the name of a rock group on it, ripped jeans and tennis shoes? Even if he had a degree from Harvard Medical School, you'd probably have doubts about everything he said to you. No matter how qualified your staff may be, prospects won't take them seriously unless they look professional. For most events, that means a suit for guys and a suit or dress for women. By the way, if you say you're going to wear a tuxedo, don't leave off the jacket. A tuxedo shirt, bow tie, and cummerbund is not a tuxedo. Spring for the jacket. It doesn't cost that much.

☐ Yes ☐ No **We pride ourselves on the way we handle incoming calls, and realize they are our greatest source of leads, new business, and customer satisfaction.**

Every incoming call is an opportunity to make a new customer. When an employee answers your phone, he or she is quarterbacking your entire company. (See chapter 5.)

☐ Yes ☐ No **I read all of the trade magazines.**

In order to serve your customers, you and your employees have to be up-to-date on the latest trends, developments, and equipment in the DJ field. Many of your customers will have done some research before meeting you. It doesn't help your em-

Customer Service as a Sales Tool

ployees if they know less than the customers do. Subscribe to all of the trade magazines and keep them at the office for your employees to read.

☐ Yes ☐ No **We have a newsletter that we send out to all of our customers and prospects at least quarterly.**

Unlike some direct mail, newsletters will usually at least get looked at before they're thrown away. A newsletter gives you another contact with customers and prospects, and keeps your name out there. It's your opportunity to highlight new packages or equipment, spotlight your employee-of-the-month and provide useful information.

☐ Yes ☐ No **We always keep our promises.**

If you don't, you'll have a difficult time increasing your business any time soon. Doing what you say you will shows integrity. Not doing what you say you will shows carelessness or worse.

☐ Yes ☐ No **We always try to find ways to make our business look different.**

What are one or two things that make you stand out from the other DJs in town?

135

☐ Yes ☐ No   We keep in touch with our loyal clients regularly with thank-you notes, customer-appreciation days, holiday cards, and private open-house events.

It costs five times as much to find new customers as it does to keep existing customers. It's easier and more cost-effective to keep your current customers happy than to court new ones. Current customers are the best source of new referrals and more business. Make them feel valued—reward them for doing business with you.

☐ Yes ☐ No   We provide an e-mail address.

It may not be that important, but having an e-mail address shows that you are aware of current technology and that you are completely accessible.

☐ Yes ☐ No   **We always show our customers how to save money, even before they ask.**

Showing your customers how they can save money when planning their event demonstrates that you care about their budgets and that you can provide what they need for a reasonable price. Everyone likes to save money.

Customer Service as a Sales Tool

☐ Yes ☐ No   **Our invoices and contracts are all clear, easy-to-read, and use very simple language.**

Long, complex agreements make many customers uncomfortable. You don't want to slow the selling process or compromise the good feelings that have built up during the process by using a complicated contract or invoice.

☐ Yes ☐ No   **We always try to make every client feel special, like each one is the most important we have.**

Personality skills are important in catering to a customer's wants and needs. When a salesperson is with a customer, that customer should be the focus of his or her attention—everything else can wait.

☐ Yes ☐ No   **We always try to do something extra for the customer.**

Go out of your way to keep customers happy: you never know how many friends they may refer to you in the future. If a customer requests a song you don't currently own, go ahead and get it. The goodwill that results will be worth more than the few dollars it cost you.

How many of the preceding questions could you honestly say "yes" to? How many of these questions strike a nerve, and remind you that with a little ingenuity and creativeness, you could increase your mobile DJ business right away? If you are saying "no" to more than three, you might want to reassess your customer service thoughts and goals.

In today's business world, customers are demanding and getting the service that they're paying for. Most customers who get poor service never do business with that company again. And they tell all of their friends to avoid it as well. But those who have a positive experience not only keep coming back for more, they send their friends to the DJ, too.

Keep in mind that the Golden Rule has to be modified if you really want to crank your sales up a notch. The Golden Rule is: "Do unto others as you would have them do unto you." You need to follow the Platinum Rule: "Do unto others as they want to be done unto." Customer service requires you to give your customers what they want, if you want them to keep coming back.

Customer Service as Insurance

When you start to think about the assets of your business, your thoughts probably go to your equipment. Insurance will replace that in case of a loss. But your greatest asset is your customer base. And insurance won't replace lost customers. The only insurance against the loss of customers is exceptional service.

Stop to think for a minute about why you go to the same dry cleaner, dentist, or hairdresser, and you'll realize that service plays a big part in your decision of where to take your business. If you're not happy, you just find someone else.

Client retention through customer service has to be seen as a profit center in your business. "Slam-dunking" customers into signing and then forgetting about them afterwards is not a long-term solution for any business. Avoiding customer complaints, not returning phone calls, treating customers like they're intrusions in your day, having minimal ethics, and less-than-adequate service are not investments in success.

There seem to be three basic standards for customer service.

1) Minimum Service: Doing just enough to get by, deterring lawsuits, and fulfilling the minimum responsibility for refunds.

2) Average Service: Giving the customer a fair exchange. Customers receive reasonable value for their dollars—no less and no more. Actually, most businesses are at this level. As a result, most businesses see average results. They generally turn a profit and stay in business during good times.

3) Maximum Service: Constantly striving to reward customers for their patronage. This means taking the ethical high ground, going the extra mile, painting an honest picture of your services, and then taking it one step beyond.

If you have employees, they need to be taught the basic principles and value of customer service. To sum it up, customer service means making buying a pleasant, easy experience for your customers. Stress to your employees that it's their job to assure that booking you for their event is a positive experience. When customers feel that they're getting great service, they won't want to go anywhere else—and they won't send their friends anywhere else either.

12

I am an optimist—it does not seem to be much use being anything else.

—Winston Churchill

Putting Your Plan into Action

Flip back to the cover of this book. Take another look at the title: "Increase Your Mobile DJ Business By 30% ... Starting Next Month!" And remember, you've already found out that you have to do something *this month* to attain that goal. Do you actually know what that goal is? Do you know what your monthly bookings total? Find out. Look it up. Now increase that number by 30 percent and write it down. Put in on a piece of paper. Stick in on your calendar. If you don't know where you're going, how will you know when you get there? How will you know if you've reached your goal or not?

Now, since you also already have a legal pad with a line drawn down the middle with a "to do" and "to call" list on either side (see chapter 1), let's write down on the bottom of the pad a few of the things you're going to do to achieve your goal.

Are you going to make those six contacts per day? Are you going to start logging every incoming call and establish a game plan for handling each one? Are you and your employees going to try for a name and appointment every time there's a customer inquiry on the phone? Are you going to start maximizing referrals, and begin trying different approaches to turning leads into sales?

You won't know if they'll work or not until you try. And if you do what you've always done, you're going to get what you've always gotten. It's time to shift gears and to try a few new ideas and approaches to finding more clients and booking more gigs.

Will it work? That depends on what you believe. If you think those new ideas and approaches for bringing in more clients will work, they will. If you think business won't get better, that things are tough, the economy is bad and customers are difficult to find, you're right as well. It's whatever you believe.

Getting more bookings is a matter of knowing what to do and how to do it ... and it's a matter of attitude as well. If you want something badly enough, there's always a way to achieve it.

How badly do you want to increase your mobile DJ business? If you want to do it badly enough, you might find that you won't even have to wait until next month for a 30 percent increase. In fact, it could start today.

Let's do it!